BIG STAR FALLIN' MAMA

"The passionate, personal music of Black America is one of this nation's greatest cultural treasures. The essence of this art, as it has been evolving over the years, is extraordinarily difficult to put into words, but Hettie Jones has done just that, and extremely well, for readers of all ages."—*New York* magazine

"Hettie Jones has written something very beautiful and important here—a book that clarifies an area of music still much misunderstood, for all of its present immediacy and vitality. Ms. Jones's five portraits are warm, touching, and richly informed."

—*The New York Times*

"Written with candor and sensitivity. . . . Gives a great deal of information about popular music in this country and the contributions of many black performing artists as well as of the five biographees." —*Bulletin of the Center for Children's Books*

"An important book. . . . Offers special insight into the African American music scene from the 1920s to the present."

—*School Library Journal*

"Each compelling story is exquisitely told, showing how an individual's life experience can effect change in a musical form."

—*The Horn Book*

"Well organized and smoothly written, the discussions of music and society are well woven into the biographical material."

—*Booklist*

BIG STAR FALLIN' MAMA

Five Women in Black Music

Revised Edition

Hettie Jones

Foreword by Nelson George

PUFFIN BOOKS

In memory of
Anna Lois Russ Jones
in 1929 the world's second fastest woman
from 1959 to 1987 the fastest grandma
and never to be out of the running

PUFFIN BOOKS
Published by the Penguin Group
Penguin Books USA Inc., 375 Hudson Street, New York, New York 10014, U.S.A.
Penguin Books Ltd, 27 Wrights Lane, London W8 5TZ, England
Penguin Books Australia Ltd, Ringwood, Victoria, Australia
Penguin Books Canada Ltd, 10 Alcorn Avenue, Toronto, Ontario, Canada M4V 3B2
Penguin Books (N.Z.) Ltd, 182-190 Wairau Road, Auckland 10, New Zealand

Penguin Books Ltd, Registered Offices: Harmondsworth, Middlesex, England

First published in the United States of America by The Viking Press, Inc., 1974
Revised edition first published by Viking, a division of Penguin Books USA Inc., 1995
Published in Puffin Books, 1997

1 3 5 7 9 10 8 6 4 2

Cover photos, from top: Billie Holiday (Columbia Records / Don Hunstein), Ma Rainey (Columbia
Records/ Don Hunstein), Mahalia Jackson (Columbia Records / Don Hunstein), Aretha Franklin
(Columbia Records / Don Hunstein), Bessie Smith (Frank Driggs / Photo Files).

Acknowledgments
From "Yes Yes Yes Yes" (published in 1961) and from "Sunshine Always Open Out" (published in
1965) by Whitney Balliett. Reprinted by permission of The New Yorker.

Pages 139–141 constitute an extension of this copyright page.

THE LIBRARY OF CONGRESS HAS CATALOGED THE VIKING EDITION AS FOLLOWS:
Jones, Hettie.
Big star fallin' mama : five women in Black music / Hettie Jones; foreword by Nelson George.
p.   cm.
Summary: Portraits of five Black women and the kind of music they sang during a period of social
change. Includes Ma Rainey, Bessie Smith, Mahalia Jackson, Billie Holiday, and Aretha Franklin.
Includes bibliographical references (p.), discography (p.), and index.
ISBN 0-670-85621-5
1. Afro-American women musicians—Juvenile literature. 2. Blues (Music)—Juvenile literature.
[1. Musicians. 2. Afro-Americans—Biography. 3. Blues (Music)] I. Title.
ML82.J65 1995 782.42'1643'092—dc20 [B] 94–33469 CIP MN

Puffin Books ISBN 0-14-037747-6
Printed in the United States of America

Contents

Foreword

The role of African American women in the molding of this nation's musical heritage has been as essential as a heartbeat. The nuance, the power, the pain and the deep passion of these voices are the building blocks of American music. Without Ma Rainey, Bessie Smith, Mahalia Jackson, Billie Holiday, and Aretha Franklin, the songs that fill the radios and CD players of today are unimaginable. There is no Mary J. Blige, Mariah Carey, Janet Jackson, or Whitney Houston without the long, vibrant tradition these earlier women created.

Hettie Jones helped open the eyes of many to this vital legacy when *Big Star Fallin' Mama* was first published in 1974. This insightful writer helped shift the discussion of our nation's music from male instrumentalists to female vocalists. Jones didn't do this with anger or bile. Her agenda is based on love. Like any good teacher she pulls together the threads of music and biography to educate about these women.

This book, then, is a tool. It is not the end of your musical journey. For if Jones has touched you, as I know she will, then you'll be drawn to the music. The best way to savor *Big Star Fallin' Mama* is with the recordings of Bessie, Billie, and the rest playing in the background. Good writing about music is always an invitation to hear good music. You hold the ticket for admission in your hands.

NELSON GEORGE

Preface to the
Revised Edition

That this book is here again is testament to the tenacity of the music it describes. When it was first published in 1974, there was very little written about the blues or the general history and progress of African American music. Twenty years later *Big Star Fallin' Mama* takes its place beside others. There are not only books but seminars and college courses to add to our knowledge and appreciation of this music. Most important, the blues is alive and well, both as a recorded music that can be studied, and one that is played in many places. Blues has gone beyond music to influence art and literature, and is often used as background in films. A contribution to the whole from African Americans, it is a distinctly American creation of which all Americans can be proud. And its descendants are everywhere—from the Africa of its origin to every other place it's ever been heard. It is my hope that the revised edition of *Big Star Fallin' Mama* will offer to new generations an introduction to the remarkable story of this music and those who play and sing it.

Much credit for this undertaking is due. First, to the late Martin Williams, for his encouragement during the writing of the first edition; to my original editor, George Nicholson, and his staff; and to Martha King, who arranged for me to submit a first proposal. I am grateful also for the appreciation extended by many librarians who have suggested the book to young people over the years. Finally, my thanks go to Eric Richards, for his assistance with the discography, and to Lisa Pliscou, editor of this new edition, for her enthusiastic embrace of the project. And all praise is due, of course, to the music, to these five women and the many others who continue to sing.

HETTIE JONES

The big star fallin',
  mama it ain't long fo day
The big star fallin',
  mama tain't long fo day
Maybe the sunshine
  'll drive these blues away

BLIND WILLIE MCTELL

The Blues, Singular and Plural

In November 1920, the General Phonograph Corporation released a recording of two Perry Bradford tunes sung by Mamie Smith. Neither artist was very well known; in fact Mamie had made the record only because another singer couldn't get to the studio. But within a month seventy-five thousand copies were sold, and in six months over half a million—a lot of sales in those early days of recording. At one dollar each, that also meant a lot of money. The people at General Phonograph were astonished, though naturally delighted. The record buyers were delighted too. Most of them were black people, who were pleased to buy a recording of Mamie Smith, who was black and sang the blues, *Crazy Blues.*

General Phonograph's competitors, not to be outdone, took immediate action. Soon hundreds of recordings by black musicians had been issued, intended for sale in black communities and referred to as "Race Records." Many were recordings of a then popular kind of black music called the blues, which in the course of time had a profound influence on American music.

1

After Mamie Smith, America went through a jazz age and a swing era, and in later years was moved by rhythm and blues, rock 'n' roll, soul, disco, and rap. But the blues, if not an absolute beginning, was where most Americans came in.

The blues—what is it, or what are they? Singular or plural, a way to sing or the way you feel? Who invented the blues, are they African or American, black or white—and why blue?

The word *blues* as a description of melancholy or a "down in the dumps" feeling was in use before the music called blues appeared. It had come into the language as a short way to say "blue devils." In England, as far back as the 1500s, "blue devils" meant an unseen but threatening group of spirits that would hover around people who felt low. They apparently emigrated, along with the rest of the English language, and plagued early Americans like Thomas Jefferson. He reported, "We have something of the blue devils at times." Some years later, in the nineteenth century, Washington Irving called his devils merely "the blues."

But having the blues, plural, and singing blues, although related, are not exactly the same. The music that came to be called blues in the singular sense has its own history; it is singular also because it is unique and extraordinary. A distinctly American music, the blues is a contribution, ironically, from the only people who became Americans against their will. It is related to African music in some ways, to European music in others. It is something like a spiritual and something like a hymn; it's a song but it's also a story. The blues, as a musician once commented, "is all by itself."

> *The blues? Why the blues are a part of*
> *me. To me, the blues are . . . like spirituals,*
> *almost sacred. When we sing blues, we're*

*singin' out our hearts, we're singin' out
our feelings.*

The African people brought to this country to be slaves knew a complicated music that westerners have begun only recently to study. African songs may have eight or nine parts, for different voices as well as for percussion, wind, and stringed instruments, somewhat like a western symphony. Also, and very important to the development of blues, in most African languages words and their meanings are so bound up with music that the language itself is a form of music—a word cannot be considered without its sound. When you speak you are singing, and the song you sing is what you mean to say. The reverse is also true: some African instruments—for example drums—were made to imitate the human voice, and therefore could "speak the same language." Music was the way people learned their history and traditions; it was essential to African life.

But Africans were brought to America without their xylophones made of gourds, their ivory trumpets and reed flutes, their talking drums. Only the voice was left, and the ear, and the knowledge of how to make an instrument—it's less difficult to make your own if you have always made your own. Slaveholders either encouraged or discouraged African music—whichever suited their convenience. Slaves were encouraged to sing because it appeared that singing "kept up their spirits," and everyone appreciated having them perform a little "Saturday evening amusement." White people watched these shows dismayed but nevertheless pleased at what they heard: "the weird, grotesque, but generally melodious music of the plantation," was one description.

But it was not at all convenient that talking drums could

summon black people and possibly call them to revolt. Virginia was the first of the states, in 1676, to prohibit the assembly of blacks by drumbeat. And although singing was never forbidden, it was another inconvenience that spirituals turned out to be messages about the underground railroad or about secret meetings in the woods:

> *Steal away, steal away, steal away to Jesus,*
> *Steal away, steal away home,*
> *I ain't got long to stay here.*

> *I can tell you by your daily walk*
> *There's a meeting here tonight.*

In general very few white people listened with the idea of understanding African music, which was based on a different scale and difficult for the untrained ear. Anyway the assumption was that African people were inferior beings and must therefore produce inferior art. The idea of song as language seems not to have been considered at all. The result of this attitude was that black people were left somewhat free to develop a new music language in English. African languages were not only discouraged but gradually became less useful, especially if people found themselves in Georgia when all the others who spoke their language had been taken to Texas. There was nothing to do but get along with English as a new way to sing African music, even if consonants had to be dropped and rhymes stretched. The music sometimes required this.

> *Trouble in love comes with me, and it sho' do grieve*
> * my min',*
> *Sometimes I feel like livin', sometimes I feel like dyin'.*

Black people also picked up and taught themselves the Irish jigs, reels, hornpipes, and English country dances that served for American popular music of the day. They learned European church hymns, which had a harmonic structure different from the African but which they were able to fit into their own music easily. They made instruments out of available materials—banjos of skin with horsehair strings, animal jawbones with rattling teeth, sticks, tubs, jugs. The total effect was an African American music through which they could communicate and express themselves.

> *My old missus dead an' gone*
> *Lef' dis niggah to blow his horn.*
>
> *Ole massa dead now, let him res'*
> *Say all things is for de bes'.*

White people came to regard slave music and "plantation shows" as superior entertainment. They even made up their own versions, blackened their faces with burnt cork, and began to offer publicly these imitations of African American music, speech, humor, and dress, which they called "minstrel shows." They shook tambourines and rattled bones, except that they hadn't really listened to the music they supposed they were copying. Musically the minstrel shows were far from the truth, to say nothing of the lyrics, which were mostly something like: "We're a happy set of darkies . . ." etc., etc. But they were the most popular entertainment of the time, even traveling to Europe.

Meanwhile black people continued to sing their own music as they could, at street meetings or at church, out in the fields or wherever they were forced to labor. Outdoors alone, some-

Juba, a famous nineteenth-century African American dancer.

Thomas Rice as "Jim Crow," a minstrel imitation of African American dancing.

one might "holler," which was something like yodeling, to keep from feeling lonely or to signal a friend in the next field. People working together would sing together, sometimes with a leader to set the pace and sing one part, for Africans had long before learned to use music for coordination and efficiency.

I been hammering────huh
All over Georgia────huh
Alabama too────huh
Alabama too────huh

How long, how long────wham!
Fo' the sun goes down────wham!
Poor boy cryin', all day long────wham!

Oh let the sun go down────hunk,
And we'll get rest────hunk
Oh let the sun go down────hunk
And we'll be blest.

During the Civil War, a lot was promised beyond freedom, like forty acres of land a family might live on as citizens, and a mule they could ride to look over their spread. But some things happened and some things didn't. In southern fields slaves had sung about becoming free. In those same fields after the war, field hands sang about the life freedom had brought them. Hungry and poor, people wandered northward, westward. They hoboed on freight trains, looking for work, fleeing unjust laws. And they sang, as they always had, to ease the pain, to pass the time, to tell a story.

Although it may have actually started before the Civil War, there now began to be heard a particular kind of music. This was a short form that could be repeated without becoming boring, a form that lent itself to as much variety as different singers might bring to it. Many of the songs cast in this mold related the sad experiences of people for whom there seemed to be no place, no certainty of home or work, and they came to be called "blues" songs. The blues are not always sad though; they're full of hope, determination, and humor. They're stories of men and women in a tough world, refusing to let it keep them down.

> *When you see me coming*
> *H'ist your window high,*
> *When you see me leaving*
> *Tuck your head and cry.*

> *I am going back to Georgia*
> *Before long, baby.*

> *Well I'm worried now,*
> *Well I won't be worried long.*
> *Well I'm worried now,*
> *Well I won't be worried long.*

At this point blues was folk music, not composed specifically to entertain, and it was for the most part improvised, that is, made up as the singer went along. Like an African language, it was closer to sung speech (the song you sing is what you mean to say) than it was to composed European music or even to European folk song. But though the words and melody might differ from song to song, each blues was improvised within a certain musical structure or framework, using a certain sequence of chords. This harmonic foundation comes from European music. There are three common frameworks, but in time one became more popular and is known now as the "classic" blues structure.

The classic blues is a very simple, easy to use musical form. Lyrics aren't hard to fit in—a first line, a second line that repeats line one, and then a third line that is an answer, or "punch line" as critic Richard Hadlock described it.

> *See see rider, see what you done done,*
> *See see rider, see what you done done,*
> *Made me love you, now your gal has come.*

In musical terms, there are twelve bars or measures alto-gether; these are divided into three sections of four bars each, giving each line of the lyric equal time. The catch is, there being no more to the framework than that, the complexities of the blues are all contained inside—like many three-room houses, all with different styles of interior decoration. Even after those three-room houses were "furnished" with standard sets of lyrics, as happened after a while, there were always different ways to sit on the furniture.

There are three other remarkable musical features in the blues. One is the "call and response" pattern of the two first lines and the answering third; this is similar to African songs and to African American work songs in which a leader sings and other people answer. The pattern sets up a kind of suspense that mounts with the repetition of the second line—by the time the third line comes the listener is expecting something! The second feature is an "interior" call and response between the singer and the accompaniment. Since the vocal line usually doesn't take up the space of the whole room—or four bars—there is time left over for the instrument to

A poster advertising a tent show around the turn of the century.

comment on what has been sung, or answer the singer. ("I just step aside and let the guitar say it," one singer explained.) The third feature is the "blue note," which is ʹsung just under, or flatter than, a note as it appears on the western musical scale, but not flat enough to be the next note down. This makes the melody turn in an unexpected way, as though the tune had shifted to another, hidden scale. Both the call and response patterns and blue notes add to the variety and complexity of the blues.

> *Goin' away baby, won't be back till fall,*
> *Goin' away baby, won't be back till fall,*
> *If I find me a new man, I won't be back at all.*

By the beginning of the twentieth century, blues could be heard wherever black people gathered to sing to each other. Undoubtedly white people, especially southerners, heard the blues too. But as always it was overheard rather than listened to, and this is partly because it was to black people their own story, their own music. They were not obliged to be clear to anyone else. American popular music up to this time had remained largely in the European tradition: marches, polkas, mazurkas, waltzes—all written down, and all to be played as written by musicians who could read music. However, at the turn of the century "ragtime," originally a black music, swept the country. An instrumental music played mostly on the piano, ragtime with its "syncopated" rhythms (normally unaccented beats are accented) was a revelation to Americans more accustomed to the sentimental ballads of light opera. And you could dance to it! Ragtime went through various stages of dilution and was passé by World War I, but it did prepare American ears for jazz.

Meanwhile the blues stayed at home, like Cinderella, while the others went to the ball. It was not even thought of as music. For most white people, to listen to the blues would have meant going to saloons and street corners on the other side of town, where they would have had to confront their "Negro problem," which not many had any particular interest in solving. Nor were people as interested in "plantation music," make-believe or real, as they had been before the Civil War. Minstrel shows with their fake "darkies" gradually went out of fashion. No one made a fuss even when "genuine Negroes," as they were described in a newspaper of the time, were allowed to join the shows. Some became famous—but even Williams and Walker,

A well-known minstrel company just after the turn of the century.

who were billed as "two real coons," always added an extra layer of brown.

However, once the minstrel show became a vehicle for black entertainers, it took on a new definition. More and more black musicians, singers, and dancers joined the minstrel circuit. For one thing, minstrelsy was a way to earn a living, one of the still very few available choices. Not that it was an easy one: black minstrels sometimes took their shows to towns that welcomed them with signs reading NIGGER, READ AND RUN, often followed by AND IF YOU CAN'T READ, RUN ANYHOW. If these travelers dared to stay it was partly because they were playing now not only to white audiences who had come to laugh *at* them, but to other black people as well. They were playing to people whose seats in the balcony had been hard earned, people for whom the song you sing is what you mean to say.

Traveling from place to place, black minstrels listened to, as well as entertained, the people who worked on the railroads they traveled and the "roughnecks" who put up the tent for the show. They heard blind guitarists, most of them street singers who also sang and played for a living. For more than twenty years before Mamie Smith's recording, black minstrels were working in shows and carnivals, theaters in small southern towns, even circuses. They did the usual minstrel routines and played popular music of the day. But how long could they sing silly jingles to audiences whose musical knowledge was historically far more complicated? Minstrels worked on the blues and brought them onstage alongside the vaudeville acts, the freaks, and the snake-oil sellers.

Though the earliest country blues singers were men, when the blues assumed their classic form it was a woman who stood there under the nighttime southern sky. She wore a necklace and earrings of gold coins and she glittered behind the kerosene footlights. But she was a heroine, not a goddess; she shared with her audience the confusion of hope and uncertainty that went along with being a black American at the turn of the century. Why were they here? What was their part in this time and place? "The train is at the station," she sang for them, "I hear the whistle blow,"

> *The train is at the station, I hear the whistle blow,*
> *I done bought my ticket, but I don't know where*
>   *I'm going.*

1

Ma Rainey

People traveled for miles to see her, because she was really someone to see. Ma Rainey was short and plump and dark and flashy. She wore diamonds in her ears, around her neck, on her head and her fingers. She wore necklaces of twenty- or fifty-dollar gold pieces, dresses embroidered with rhinestones and sequins. Everyone who saw her or knew her agreed that she wasn't very pretty, but this never mattered. "She was really an ugly woman, but when she opened her mouth—that was it! You forgot everything." "Her heart was so big it made her beautiful."

It's the big heart, the sincerity, that comes through more than half a century later, despite scratchy recordings that weren't made until she was in her late thirties and had been singing for twenty years. In the photographs you can see it in her eyes, in the warm smile. You can hear it also in her voice, which comes on easily and without strain. She sounds like a lady who liked singing and liked living, and who did both with good humor and style.

Ma Rainey was the first of the great blues singers. Though for the most part her songs were her own or composed by other musicians, they were a people's stories too, like folk music. She sang of lonely women, violent or troubled women. She took their blues and used them. So much of life had been left out of minstrel music. For herself and for the others who learned from her, Ma Rainey made blues the way to begin putting it all back in.

> *He-ey jailer, tell me what have I done*
> *Ey hey jailer, tell me what have I done*
> *You got me all bound and chained, [for I killed that*
> *woman's son.]**

> *Cause I'm in prison, cause I'm in jail*
> *Cause I'm in prison, cause I'm in jail,*
> *Cold iron bars all around me, no one to go my bail.*

> *I've got a mother and father, livin' in a cottage by*
> *the sea*
> *Got a mother and father, livin' in a cottage by the sea,*
> *Got a sister and brother, wonder do they think of*
> *poor me.*

Ma Rainey's voice has been equated with the "black" in "black is beautiful." Into the slapstick humor of a minstrel song she put blues notes and moans. She took many of the features of field hollers and spirituals and incorporated them into her style, so that even songs that weren't blues came off with a bluesy feeling. In so doing she pioneered a new popular music,

---

*Words unclear in recording.

18

taking the blues out of the back room and off the street corner and letting them strut their stuff on the stage.

> *You can have my money baby, everything I own*
> *But for god's sake leave my man alone*
> *Cause I'm jealous, jealous hearted me,*
> *I'm just jealous, jealous as I can be.*

> *It takes a rockin' chair to rock, a rubber ball to roll,*
> *Takes the man I love to satisfy my soul*
> *Cause I'm jealous, jealous hearted me,*
> *I'm just jealous, jealous as I can be.*

The earliest country blues singers, who were almost always men, usually knew one or two songs on which they would improvise variations to fit the town they were in or the occasion for singing. Variety in their lyrics or melodies was not what made their music interesting or worth listening to—it was the emotion they conveyed. "The blues came from nothingness, from want, from desire," was one explanation. Ma Rainey knew where blues came from; like many others she could sing about the things that were troubling her. Black folk music was her heritage. The difference was that she was a singer by profession and by trade, and she could express these feelings with style, and with more than a usual amount of skill. Apparently it was a skill that appeared early. Her brother told an interviewer that her talent for singing was evident even when she was quite young. Another person called her "a child prodigy in her time."

Born Gertrude Pridgett on April 27, 1886, in Columbus, Georgia, Ma Rainey was the second of Thomas and Ella Allen Pridgett's five children. The Pridgetts had come to Georgia from Alabama. Columbus was a port on the Chattahoochee

River, a shipping center and industrial town of some seven thousand people the year of Gertrude's birth, about half of them black. Her family settled in Columbus, and though Gertrude lived a wandering life it remained her town, the place to come back to, home.

> *I'm a common old rollin' stone*
> *Just got the blues for home sweet home,*
>   *Yes, suh!*
> *I'm an old rollin' stone*
> *Just got the blues for home sweet home.*

Not much is known of Gertrude's childhood. No doubt she heard kids beating on tin pans and milk pails and singing through combs, as they did in the country South in those days. She probably heard people singing to the rhythm of nails rattling the loose teeth of a mule jawbone, and heard the music of washtub bass fiddles, and jugs that sounded like tubas. (Later in life, she recorded with jug bands, and she was always fond of their "country" sound.) As a young girl she was baptized in the First African Baptist Church, where there was certainly music to be heard. Her hometown, which only a lifetime before had been a Creek Indian village, was by then a bustling city. You can sail the Chattahoochee all the way to the Gulf of Mexico, and like other inland river ports in the South, Columbus had its share of travelers from afar, sophistication, theater. One of Gertrude's grandmothers had been on the stage in the years "after surrender," as people called it, after the Civil War.

Columbus was a regular stop on the minstrel circuit, which meant that fiddles and other western-style instruments could be heard when the "musicianers" came to town. It was large and prosperous enough to support the Springer Opera House, where in 1900 at the age of fourteen Gertrude Pridgett began her singing career in a talent show called the Bunch of Blackberries. She must have followed that first show with further performances because sometime during the next few years William "Pa" Rainey took notice of her—he was a minstrel show manager—and on February 2, 1904, Gertrude became at once Mrs. Rainey and the star of the Rabbit Foot Minstrels. Though she had no children and acquired the title while still a little young for it, Gertrude was "Ma" to Will's "Pa" from then on. It seemed to suit her. According to people who worked with her, she "was always doing nice things and taking everyone as if they were her own kids."

With her new husband, eighteen-year-old Ma Rainey began the travels that lasted for nearly thirty-five years and took her everywhere in the South, to the Midwest, even to Mexico. The routines of the Raineys were at first not especially new—they included some dancing and humorous conversation as well as singing:

> [Knock knock knock knock]
> *Who's that knockin' on that door?*
> *It's me, baby.*
> *Me who?*
> *Well you know I'm your wife.*
> *Whaa?   Wife?*
> *Yeh!*
> *Ain't that awful? I don't let no woman quit me*
>   *but one time.*
> *I just quit one little old time, just one time!*

The Rabbit Foot show also had its assortment of freaks, comedians, and acrobats. Featured at one time were the com-

An advertisement for a 1920s show featuring Ma Rainey— which misspelled her name..

edy team of Skeeter and Lil Liz, a juggler named John Pamplin who also did a Faust act and rattled a big iron ball, and Delamon Miles, who according to a contemporary description was "a contortionist who could turn himself around completely and he was quite baffling to the people in that he was able to move around and walk backwards with his feet turned in opposite directions."

But along with the acts came the band. Musicians were very important for a number of reasons. They of course played behind most of the acts, and they would also parade into the center of each little town early on the day of the show in order to advertise. Sometimes the audience would march back to the tent right behind the band, so caught up were they with the music! A good band was very good for business. But even more important, if Ma Rainey was the fairy godmother who dressed up the blues and brought them to the ball, she was certainly lent a hand by some of the South's best musicians. Later on, many became famous as the first jazz artists of the twentieth century. At this time, though, before recordings, the minstrel circuit provided employment at decent salaries, and a place where musicians could learn from each other and practice—a training ground. Many of them divided their time between minstrel shows and work in New Orleans; as the guitarist Danny Barker remembered: "You would see a cat disappear, you would wonder where he was, and finally somebody would say that he'd left for one of the shows, that they had sent for him."

Ma Rainey appeared not only with the Rabbit Foot show, but with others like Tolliver's Circus and Musical Extravaganza, the C. W. Parks Minstrels, Silas Green's. These shows spent winters in New Orleans, where Ma would appear in alley tent shows. She employed local musicians who also played the saloons and dance halls in Storyville, New Orleans' famous red light district, and in the marching and brass bands that city was famous for. She knew Joe "King" Oliver, who was Louis Armstrong's teacher (Armstrong appeared later on some of her records), and others who were working on blues and jazz. Some musicians were readers, many just "faked it" or played by ear, but they all learned from one another, developing their music language on instruments like the trumpet, trombone, clarinet, tuba, and, later, the saxophone. They perfected the call-and-response pattern between voice and instrument in the classic blues. The traveling show was a perfect medium for this. After all, if you travel with some people for periods of time, living with them in a railroad car, going from every little town to every bigger town and back again, you're bound to have a few things to say, musically as well as any other way. "Don't play that band, mister, just play the blues for me!" Ma Rainey orders on *Slow Drivin' Moan.*

The minstrels were quite a traveling crew: musicians, singers, acrobats, and freaks, plus the roustabouts, all packed into railroad cars, one side for the tent and one side for the personnel. And how they did travel! As Charles Love described, "We'd be in a country town like on a Saturday night . . . on Sunday we'd walk around and see the sights; then move on. Next place, Monday, they'd put the tent up." Everybody listened to everybody else:

> *Fellers puttin' up the tents they had their own little*
> *songs you know. . . . They'd be singing and we'd be*
> *laughing, looking at them. . . . They would sing a song as*
> *they pulled the ropes and got the tent up—they were the*
> *same like railroad songs and the way them roustabouts*
> *on the steamboats, they sing a lot of that stuff too.*

Then the musicians could entertain the work crew:

*So by the time they had the sides on all the way round
and got that in good the band would go in and if they
had to practice anything they would do it in the tent.*

The minstrels had come to entertain the people, but the people
also played and sang for the minstrels. Brother John Sellers,
who became a singer himself, remembered how exciting it all
was when he was a child:

*When they put up the big tent I used to slip on out and
watch the show—lift up the edge of the canvas. Then
they used to have talent competitions sometimes and I
was just a kid but I would sing too. . . . And then I could
see the show from the inside. It wasn't only blues you
know, they'd have comedians and dancers and so forth
like that but I always did remember the blues singers
best. That's how I first heard Ma Rainey. . . . They had a
stage up there with curtains and everything and then
these would open and some big woman would be hol-
lerin' there.*

Looking back, it seems natural that Ma Rainey, in a situation
like that of the minstrel show, would begin to include the blues
as a regular presentation. Someone as kind and generous as
she would have wanted to communicate with her audiences in
a special way. Ma Rainey liked people, and her audiences
were *her* people. Columbus was home, but the entire South
was her territory, and her care for people well known. ("Ma
Rainey is sponsoring a midnight ramble this week in Nashville
Tenn. for the benefit of the flood sufferers in Alabama. It is just
like big-hearted Ma Rainey to do this humane thing.") For Ma
the diamonds and sequined dresses were theatrical magic; she

did not wear them in the street. She was a hard-working woman who often worked and lived outdoors, and she sang to others who spent their days laboring outdoors, sometimes in the same fields where the minstrels pitched their tents. Ma Rainey performed in barns and schoolhouses and dance halls as well as in theaters. Dressing rooms, if there were any, were not exactly luxurious. Hers was not the comfortable life of a movie star; she wasn't a glamor girl, a beauty queen. People called her Ma or Mother or Mama out of respect, and they loved her. She came to *their* communities, to their vacant lots and schoolhouses. She knew how they lived because in large part that was also the way she lived.

It was a different world they shared then—difficult, full of the private hardships peculiar to the black community, and isolated, like the world of many other Americans as well. Most people had not yet felt the effects of the Industrial Revolution. There were few automobiles and few telephones. There was no radio or television. One didn't always get to turn on a faucet; indoor plumbing was still for the rich, even in cities. Roads were dirt roads. Railroads carried people long distances, but they were a long day's journey and a lot of chugging and bumping. Hardly anyone could afford to travel. For black people, information didn't travel easily either; few newspapers were distributed in the black communities of the South. "I did a kind of bootleg business in Northern Negro newspapers and magazines," wrote W. C. Handy, another musician of that time.

> *Not only did I supply the colored folks of the town, but also got the trade of the farmers, the croppers and the hands from the outlying country. They would come to my house on their weekly visits to the city, give me the high sign, and I would slip them their copies of the* Chicago

Defender, *the* Indianapolis Freeman *or the* Voice of the
Negro. . . . *I was venturing into risky business. Negro
newspapers were not plentiful in those days, and their
circulation in cities like Clarksdale [Miss.] was looked
upon with strong disfavor by certain of the local powers.*

Moreover, the situation in the South remained not only separate but blatantly unequal. For every eighty cents the state of
Georgia spent on a white child's education, it spent twenty on
the black child. "Colored" schools were often open no more
than two or three months of the year. Colleges like Tuskegee
Institute were training young men to farm and shoe horses and
young women to cook and make brooms—all skills that would
have no place in the industrial world that was on its way.
When the South built factories, black men became the janitors.

For those whose anger could not be contained, who could not
bring themselves to always use the back door, life was dangerous. More than one hundred people were lynched *every year* in
the first years of the twentieth century. The law offered no pro-
tection as well as no advantage. And the chain gang was *real.*
Ma Rainey sang:

> *The judge found me guilty, the clerk he wrote it down
> The judge found me guilty, the clerk he wrote it down,
> Just a poor gal in trouble, I know a county road's now.*
>
> *Many days of sorrow, many nights of woe
> Many days of sorrow, many nights of woe,
> And a ball and chain, everywhere I go.*
>
> *It was early this morning that I had my trial
> It was early this morning that I had my trial,*

> *Ninety days on the county road, and the judge*
> *didn't even smile.*

People subjected to this kind of oppression had no way to express their anger. They had to make do any way they could, sometimes mistreating one another because they had only each other, but somehow they managed to retain their humor, the ability to let the lid off through comedy.

> *Lord it ain't no maybe about my man bein' rough,*
> *Lord it ain't no maybe about my man bein' rough,*
> *But when it comes to lovin', he sure can strut his stuff.*

Ma Rainey and her Georgia Jazz Band in concert about the time of World War I.

*You 'buse me and mistreat me, you throw me round
    and beat me
Still I'm gonna hang around,
Take all my money, black up both of my eyes,
Give it to another woman, come home and tell me lies,
You low down alligator, just watch me soon or later,
Gonna catch you with your britches down!*

Many people packed up and headed North or West—better to leave home than endure the poverty and restraint imposed on them in the South. And there was work in the North, especially at the time of World War I. But for those who stayed through that time the South changed few of its ways, and black people still had to play the game of happy darky. They could have their music and their fun, as long as they kept their mouths shut and swept up.

When the recording company's talent scouts found Ma Rainey in 1924, Paramount advertised with a big headline: "Discovered at Last—MA RAINEY—Mother of the Blues." How amusing it must have been to Gertrude Pridgett Rainey after all those years—to be "discovered" at thirty-eight when she was already a legend among her own people, being "found" as though she had been living in obscurity!

But she went to New York and to Chicago and we are fortunate that she made about ninety records. Anyone can listen to her "Eh-hey-eh-eh-e boweevil" and hear a field holler—an African sound transported to America, a countryside sound that recalls a nearly forgotten past. Ma Rainey tended to slur her words (most country singers did) and all her recordings were made before Paramount had electric equipment; the combination makes for difficult understanding. But her voice is

friendly and compelling; she is funny sometimes and sometimes very, very sad.

> *I'm a lone boweevil, been out a great long time*
> *I'm a lone boweevil, been out a great long time,*
> *I'm gonna sing these blues so even boweevil knows*
>   *they're mine.*

> *Lord I feel that trouble rising with the sun*
> *Lord I feel my trouble rising with the sun,*
> *Cause that low down dirty, is lovin' some other one.*

Ma Rainey went North to sing in person after she had
become known there through her recordings. But it was
another world; she felt strange and out of place in the city.
Mary Lou Williams, the jazz pianist, remembered seeing her
in Pittsburgh:

> *The fabulous Ma Rainey came into a little theater on*
> *Wiley Avenue. Some of the older kids and I slipped*
> *downtown to hear the woman who had made blues*
> *history.*
> *Ma was loaded with real diamonds . . . her hair was*
> *wild and she had gold teeth. What a sight! To me, as a*
> *kid, the whole thing looked and sounded weird.*

The audiences up North were her children gone into a new
life; they had been made strangers by the coldness, the hard-
ness of cities. Ma Rainey's home and her heart were down
South. She continued to tour until 1935, when she returned to
Columbus after her sister Malissa died, to live in the house she
had built for her family. A good businesswoman, she had

bought two theaters in the nearby city of Rome, which she operated from then on. By the age of fifty she no longer sang regularly. She joined the Friendship Baptist Church, where her brother Thomas Pridgett, Jr., was a deacon. Three days before Christmas in 1939 Ma Rainey died. The death certificate gives her occupation as housekeeping.

Lord I'm going to sleep now, just now I got bad news
Lord I'm going to sleep now, just now I got bad news,
Ah to dream away my troubles, ah countin' these blues.

If anybody ask you who wrote this lonesome song
Tell 'em you don't know the writer, but Ma Rainey
    put it on.

2

Bessie Smith

They called her the Empress of Blues, although unlike most royalty no one is sure when she was born, or until recently even certain of how she died. But there are different ways to consider a life: that she has been and gone is one thing, that she left us her soul is another. Bessie Smith was a big woman, two hundred pounds and nearly six feet tall, with a great big voice and a colossal style. Yet it wasn't that she was large or loud that made the difference. Great art is noticeable, and Bessie was a great artist. By the time she was known there were lots of blues singers around, some of them good and many of them named Smith. But as Alberta Hunter told it, and she was a blues singer herself, "Bessie Smith was the greatest of them all. There never was one like her and there'll never be one like her again. Even though she was raucous and loud, she had a sort of a tear—no, not a tear, but there was a *misery* in what she did. It was as though there was something she had to get out, something she just had to bring to the fore."

Bessie's private miseries might have been cause enough for

her being able to sing blues, though there is more to her genius than that. She was born in Chattanooga, Tennessee, before the turn of the century (once she gave April 15, 1894, as the date but there are no birth records). Her family was poor—very poor, which usually meant very hungry, among other things. Soon after she was born her father William, a part-time Baptist preacher, died. Two brothers also died, and her mother Laura lived only until Bessie was nine. After Mrs. Smith's death the six living children—Viola, Bessie, Tinnie, Lulu, Andrew, and Clarence—had to manage by themselves. Bessie had been going to school but that ended, since going to school was hardly a consideration when you had to figure out a way to eat, right away. For young black girls in the South at that time there were not that many choices: lacking any special talent, you could mind children, clean houses, or wash other people's dirty clothes all day and sometimes half the night for three dollars a month. More than that and you were lucky. As a street singer complained: "My girl's a housemaid and she earns a dollar a week / I'm so hungry on payday I cain't hardly speak."

But Bessie was lucky. Bessie could sing. With her brother Andrew on guitar, she began singing for small change on the streets of Chattanooga. Then Clarence, a dancer-comedian, joined the Moses Stokes minstrel show and got his sister an audition. Ma and Pa Rainey were also with the Stokes company at that time, and a few months later Bessie began appearing with them in another show, not far away in Georgia. Though many legends later surrounded their relationship, Clarence's wife Maud reported that the Raineys never kidnapped Bessie, as was once thought. Nor did Ma teach Bessie how to sing, though she did mother her. In any case, the two remained fond of each other, even after Bessie went off on her own.

Aside from the pleasure of it or the glamor, as a professional singer Bessie at least had a chance. In 1913 she was making ten dollars a week at the 81 Theater. She appeared with Pete Werley's Florida Cotton Blossoms and other traveling shows, and made the usual one-night stands and weekly bookings on the minstrel circuit. For more than five years she was a regular feature of the T.O.B.A., the Theater Owners Booking Association (also known as Tough on Black Artists [or Asses]). All over the South people soon knew of her. Had she lived and sung even a few years earlier, her life would have remained, as Ma Rainey's had, intimately involved with the South, with the people of Clarksdale, Natchez, Birmingham, Atlanta, and all the little towns in between.

But this was not to be the case, not only because different lives have different goals, or because Ma had a home in the South and Bessie did not, though both of these are true. One is always, even if isolated, a part of the life of the times. And times were changing. Very rapidly the twentieth century began to make itself known as an era of unprecedented change.

For black people the North called—jobs and money and supposedly a chance to realize the American dream as had the immigrant groups from Europe. Even if you were black you could make five dollars a day putting together cars in Mr. Ford's factory. There was now a northern black culture, very much influenced by the city and by industry, by constant interaction with the white world. Ragtime was no longer popular; the blues lay behind in the South. But more and more that influence was felt as people went North, music with them in their heads, people from New Orleans, St. Louis, and southern country places. They went to Philadelphia, to Newark, to Harlem, to the South Side of Chicago that Mahalia Jackson told about:

When I first saw it, getting off the train from New Orleans, the South Side was a Negro city. It had Negro policemen and firemen and schoolteachers. There were Negro doctors and lawyers and aldermen. . . . You could go for miles and miles without seeing a white person. The South Side, like Harlem, was the place the Negro went home to after working to earn his money in other parts of the city. When he got there he could lay down his burden of being a colored person in the white man's world and lead his own life.

Bessie went North to Atlantic City, a town very popular with musicians and sophisticated audiences from the northern cities. She spent the year 1920 there, playing with jazz musicians on a bill that also included some famous names in the black entertainment world. That was also the year the recording business reluctantly made room for Mamie Smith, and after finding her to be a gold mine rushed to find other black singers.

Though record players and records of one sort or another had been on the market since 1888, recording companies weren't exactly thriving. A number of them had been in business since around the turn of the century, competing to record opera singers and other musical celebrities. Apart from some 1902 recordings by the Dinwiddie Colored Quartet (advertised as "genuine Jubilee and Camp Meeting Shouts sung as only negroes can sing them"), and groups like the Fisk Jubilee Singers who offered spirituals only, black musicians had been absent from the catalogues. Popular singers, even those who began to sing imitations of blues, were always white. "What

Bessie,
portrait from around 1920.

the white man in New York called the blues," said clarinetist Garvin Bushell in a *Jazz Review* interview, "was just more ragtime." The companies' continued refusal to record black musicians caused resentment in black communities, where many families had phonographs and were eager to hear recordings by their favorite artists.

Mamie was advertised as a "singer of 'Blues'—the music of so new a flavor," though she wasn't strictly a blues singer but a pop vaudeville artist who sometimes sang blues. After her success there was no lack of available recordings. During 1921 and 1922 an average of one record a week by black women singers was issued, and every company had its stars: Mamie, Trixie, and Clara Smith (not related), Alberta Hunter, Edith Wilson, Lucille Hegamin, Ethel Waters, and many others. Most of them, like Mamie, leaned more toward a popular style. Describing someone he worked with, Garvin Bushell explained, "She wasn't like Bessie, and . . . using Bessie as your definition, she wasn't a blues singer." But many sang well, some with a lyric grace like Sippie Wallace (the Texas Nightingale) and others with more of the "shout," like Bessie.

That all of a sudden everyone was recording blues singers hadn't made much difference for Bessie. She auditioned for three companies and they all turned her down. Too loud, they said, not refined enough. Thomas Edison, who owned one company, thought her voice was "no good." Recording wasn't quite ready for Bessie. The blues as she sang them were considered low-down and dirty: "lower class" to the respectable, "devil music" to the religious. They were also known as "gutbucket blues," after the bucket of chitterlings or hog guts available from slaughterhouses whenever you had no money for anything else. Blues weren't heard in most middle-class black homes, where the idea was to set aside this musical memory of Africa and of slavery. Many people believed that by accepting certain white-approved standards they would obtain justice for themselves and their children. But standards for behavior sometimes obscured artistic standards: Bessie failed her test for Black Swan Records because she interrupted

Bessie doing the Charleston.

a song with "Hold on; let me spit!" The president of the company immediately ended the audition.

Disappointed by her failure to record, Bessie returned to the South and to touring during 1921 and 1922. At the end of 1922, however, Columbia Records appointed a new man to be in charge of recording "race material." "The Race" was a term black people used; whites more often said "colored people." The description "Race Records" wasn't used regularly until 1923; it referred specifically to those records made for black audiences, listed separately in record catalogues and not often available in stores in white communities. Frank Walker, Columbia's new man, had spent some time listening to music, and he had as his advisor from the black music world a friend and promoter of Bessie, Clarence Williams, who often accompanied her on the piano and with whom she had sometimes traveled. Walker himself had also heard Bessie sing in a bar in Selma, Alabama, when she was only a teenager. He mentioned later that he had never heard anyone like her. Disregarding reports that others had found her manner too coarse and her voice too rough, Walker sent Williams to bring her up to New York (she was then appearing successfully in Philadelphia). Walker's response, when Bessie arrived at the studios: "The girl he brought back looked like anything *but* a singer. She looked about seventeen—tall and fat and scared to death—just awful! But all of this you forgot when you heard her sing."

> *Trouble, trouble, I've had it all my days*
> *Trouble, trouble, I've had it all my days*
> *It seems that trouble's going to follow me to my grave.*

Between February and June 1923, Walker made eighteen "sides" of Bessie, most of them with only piano accompaniment. The first to be released—*Downhearted Blues / Gulf Coast Blues*—was a fantastic success. Even though *Downhearted Blues* had already been recorded by other singers, Bessie's version sold three quarters of a million copies.

After that, there were some good times for Bessie. She fell in love, and was married in June to Jackie Gee, a Philadelphia policeman. She was being paid $125 per side for her records. The demand for her personal appearances grew. During the summer she toured the South, in the fall made more records, next winter was on the radio, then went to Chicago. "I stood in line to hear Bessie Smith at the Avenue Theater," Mahalia Jackson remembered, "and sat in my seat so thrilled to hear her as she filled the whole place with her voice that I never went home until they put us out and closed up for the night." "A voice that will never be mistaken for another's . . . in a class by herself in the field of 'blues,'" a newspaper raved.

That's what it was about Bessie—as a singer, she had no equal. One of the first American writers to consider blues and jazz called her voice "immense." That is close. Like an opera singer, her voice was full and rich. Though they called her a "shouter," she didn't yell, she always sang. Like the field hollers or shouts that her sound was descended from, her blues are musical calls—you can't shout them any more than you can shout a yodel. She could sing pretty nearly anything to some effect, and did—popular songs as well as blues. She could take the ordinary words of an ordinary song and alter their meaning and their emotional intent through time and tone. Musically, she always knew what she was doing, and she rarely made mistakes. "She would get an idea, then we would discuss it," Frank Walker explained. "But once she started to sing, nobody told her what to do. Nobody interfered." Unlike the slurred words of the country singers, Bessie's lyrics were pronounced with great care; most of the time every word she sang was perfectly clear. She would hit a note exactly where she chose to—right square in the middle of it, or starting from below and sliding up, or from above and slipping down. Many other singers copied her style of dragging over a word or syllable into the next bar. Sometimes, in almost any line but especially in the repeated second line of a blues, she stopped for breath in entirely unexpected places and carried over in unexpected places. The effect of that is indescribable, a little like hearing a word in a new way that adds to one's understanding of it. Like Louis Armstrong, Bessie was a very original and influential musician.

Within a short time, record buyers had demonstrated their approval of this fantastic voice by buying two million records, more than any other Columbia artist had ever sold, and sales that were largely responsible for bringing the company out of bankruptcy. Most of these records were bought by black people; Bessie was largely unknown in white communities in the North, though she would sometimes appear for "whites only" audiences in the South. As the twenties wore on, however, some young white musicians became interested in jazz and began to play imitations, and eventually their own versions. They of course went to see Bessie, around Chicago especially. Bix Beiderbecke, one of the most notable and talented of them, is said to have once thrown his whole week's pay at Bessie's feet, just to keep her singing. White artists and writers learned of Bessie through contact with their black counterparts, the artists of the Negro Renaissance; one who went to see her came back rhapsodizing about "the powerfully magnetic personality of this elemental conjure woman with her plangent African voice, quivering with passion and pain." Another urged his readers to buy recordings: "Listening to race records," he wrote, "is nearly the only way for white people to share the Negroes' pleasure without bothering the Negroes." Columbia billed Bessie as "The Empress of Blues," but she was more commonly referred to as the Queen. "Wherever blues are sung," read the Columbia brochure, "there will you hear the name of Bessie Smith, best loved of all the Race's great blues singers."

Records spread her popularity but it was her overwhelming stage presence that affected people most: "Bessie Smith really hits 'em in Nashville. . . . She knocked all the tin off the theatre." "Bessie Smith was a fabulous deal to watch. . . . When you went to see Bessie and she came out, that was it." "She had a high-voltage magnet for a personality." People said she didn't move much while on stage, except for simple gestures of the arm or hand. She had no need for the megaphone other singers used to make themselves heard in large theaters. "When Bessie Smith sang in a theater," Langston Hughes wrote, "you could sometimes hear her . . . all up and down the street." She moved gracefully, as large people do when they are at ease with their bodies and aware of their beauty. She knew how to dress to best advantage. In the early 1920s she sometimes wore turbans of beaded satin and ostrich feathers, a silk shawl with long fringes draped from her shoulders nearly to the floor; later she wore simple gowns and not much jewelry. Bessie was elegant. "Now there was a woman!" the musician Zutty Singleton said. "I mean Bessie Smith was ALL woman! . . . She looked like a queen up there . . . with that beautiful bronze color and stern features."

So Bessie reigned, and the money poured in. And she spent it as fast as she could. She took care of her family, brought them to Philadelphia, bought a farm in New Jersey. She bought a luxurious railroad car, named it the *Jackie Gee,* and traveled the old tent show circuit with a big extravaganza. She went through

Bessie in one of her fabulous costumes.

all the little towns in the South, places where most black people remained poor and landless, citizens who still could not vote, subject as much to natural disaster as to economic deprivation.

> *Mississippi River, what a fix you left me in*
> *Mississippi River, what a fix you left me in*
> *Mudholes of water clear up to my chin*
>
> *House without a steeple, didn't even have a door*
> *House without a steeple, didn't even have a door*
> *Plain old two-room shanty but it was home sweet home*
>
> *Ma and Pa got drownded, Mississippi you're to blame*
> *Ma and Pa got drownded, Mississippi you're to blame*
> *Mississippi River, I can't stand to hear your name!*

But Bessie herself was no longer a country girl, she had moved to Philadelphia. And time as well as changing taste had altered the general content of her blues and sometimes their strict classic structure. Bessie sang a woman's lament, about love and sex, about good and bad men, as did most of the popular blues singers who recorded. Their blues were full of references to city things, to the artifacts of the twentieth century: "I had a man for fifteen years, gave him his room and board / Once he was like a Cadillac, now he's like an old worn-out Ford." The troubles of the South which gave rise to the country blues were an old story. They had become black people's history, stories to sing the same way other people recited their legends. Nostalgia for the South was part of the new city life; it was a good land even if it hadn't been theirs, it was spacious and known, and they had their own names for things there:

Ever since Miss Susie Johnson lost her jockey Lee
There's been much excitement and more to be,
You can hear moanin', moanin' night and morn,
She's wonderin' where her easy rider's gone.

Cablegram goes off in inquiry
Telegram goes off in sympathy
Letters came from down in Bam
Everywhere that Uncle Sam
(Is the ruler of delivery)*

All day the phone rings, it's not for me
At last good tidings fills my heart with glee
This message came from Tennessee:

Dear Sue, your easy rider struck this burg today
On a southbound rattler beside the pullman car
I seen him there and he was on the hog.

Oh you easy rider
Got to stay away
He had to vamp it but the hike ain't far,
He's gone where the Southern cross the Yellow Dog.**

The place "where the Southern cross the Yellow Dog" existed
for those who sang it and those who heard it sung, and they

---

*Actual words are: "Has the Rural Free Delivery."
***The place, at Moorhead, Mississippi, where the north-south railroad line meets
the east-west Yazoo Delta (nicknamed the Yellow Dog). The song Bessie
recorded was written by W. C. Handy, but the last line is a very old blues line
that he incorporated into his version.*

understood phrases like "easy rider," "southbound rattler," and "on the hog." Bessie recorded *Yellow Dog Blues* with Fletcher Henderson and His Hot Six, a group composed of some of the best jazz musicians of the time, and the progress of their song is like a trip down South through music. But they all knew that wherever they were going, they weren't going back there. The cities were the only places to be, for musicians or for anyone who wanted a taste of the twenties.

And Bessie was the epitome of the fabulous twenties—beautiful, talented, famous, rich. But prosperity isn't always the cure if one's soul is ailing; anyway for Bessie it wasn't. Frank Walker said Bessie lived the blues, "from the time she got up in the morning until she went to bed at night," and that though she could laugh, "it didn't last long." So she drank to ease her personal miseries, a habit she'd started young, and then the drinking became a misery in itself. "Sometimes, after she'd been drinking awhile, she'd get like there was no pleasing her," Walker said. "She had this trouble in her, this thing that wouldn't let her rest sometimes, a meanness that came and took her over."

> *Stay 'way from me cause I'm in my sin*
> *Stay 'way from me cause I'm in my sin*
> *If this place gets raided it's me and my gin*

> *Any bootlegger sure is a pal of mine*
> *Any bootlegger sure is a pal of mine*
> *Cause a good old bottle of gin will get it*
> * all the time.*

Eventually even old friends began to refuse to work with her. She had marital troubles, and she was throwing money around

St. Louis Blues.

more than ever—another habit she had started young: the first eight dollars she'd earned as a kid had gone for a pair of roller skates instead of to her hungry family; she had gotten a beating from her mother for this extravagance.

The temper of the times did nothing to discourage Bessie, either: most people who could were living high then, drinking bootleg liquor (Prohibition was in effect all during the twenties) and spending money like it was going out of style. Unfortu-

Bessie with Jimmie Mordecai as her lover.

nately it was soon to be out of reach, when the stock market crashed in October 1929. But meanwhile the music went on, radio grew, and movies were all the rage. Black movie audiences were sometimes treated to strange versions of their lives on film; Bessie starred in one made during the summer of 1929. The film was called *St. Louis Blues* and that was the only song she sang in it—with a forty-two-voice chorus in the background.

I hate to see that evenin' sun go down
I hate to see that evenin' sun go down
It makes me think I'm on my last go-round

She danced a little, too, but for the most part, it's a terrible movie. Bessie wears a dress she would never have worn and some excuse for a hat. But her voice is so strong with no apparent effort that she seems to *be* the song. Watching her in this film you can understand why everyone spoke of the sight of her as well as her voice. Behind but coming through any-way, through the awful costumes and the film's misguided atti-tudes, there is Bessie, an incredibly beautiful black woman radiating life and pride. *St. Louis Blues* may still occasionally be seen on television.

Judging from this film performance, Bessie might have made a fine actress, like her contemporary and sometime rival Ethel Waters. But good times were changing to bad times. Bessie, like everyone else, was caught as the country fell more and more into the Great Depression. She made a few recordings—good ones—in 1930 and 1931. But people without jobs and money couldn't buy records or pay to see their favorite singers. The era of classic blues was over, Bessie's marriage was over (she and Jackie Gee had separated for good in 1930), and all the big money was gone.

Once I lived the life of a millionaire
Spending my money I didn't care
I carried my friends out for a good time
Buyin' bootleg liquor, champagne and wine.
Then I began to fall so low
I didn't have a friend and no place to go
But if I ever get my hands on a dollar again

I'm gonna hold on to it till them eagles grin.

Nobody knows you when you're down and out
In my pocket not one penny
And my friends I haven't any.
But if I ever get on my feet again
Then I'll meet my long lost friends
It's mighty strange without a doubt,
Nobody knows you when you're down and out,
I mean when you're down and out.

From then on Bessie sang when and where she could. Columbia dropped her contract; she made no records for the next two years. When she was asked to record again in 1933 she refused to sing the blues but did instead some vaudeville songs with a new type of band. Its sound came from a different world, not the jazz age but the swing era, and, to indicate the extent of the change, some of the musicians were white and some of them had never even seen Bessie before. But the Columbia Recording Company was bankrupt again and this time she couldn't save it, nor could it save her.

Oh me, oh my, wonder what will my end be?
Oh me, oh my, wonder what will become of poor me?
I'm standin' and thinkin' of the days gone by
I'm too weak to stand and too strong to cry

For the rest of her life Bessie worked hard trying to earn a living, mostly in New York, though she didn't appear very often. She was by this time living with Richard Morgan, uncle of the later famous jazz musician Lionel Hampton, and they got along well. "Richard was everything that Jack should have been. . . . He was perfect for Bessie, he understood her," Maud Smith recalled. Bessie now sang more pop tunes than blues, but she could still command an audience. In 1935 she was featured at the Apollo, and the owner remembered that audiences never failed to respond to her. Replacing the up-and-coming Billie Holiday (who had been taken ill) at a midtown Manhattan club, Bessie was so well received that she was held over even after a six-week engagement. A reporter interviewed her in 1937 and she seemed optimistic; things were beginning to happen again, possibilities of recording, perhaps another film. But in September of that year Bessie was killed in a car accident near Clarksdale, Mississippi, on her way to sing with a show. For many years people believed she could have been saved, that she died because she was refused medical attention

A New York nightclub where Bessie sang in her later years.

The Empress.

at a "whites only" hospital. However, the doctor who attended her at the scene of the accident, found and interviewed in 1969, stated that she had been too badly hurt to live.

"Bessie Smith was a kind of roughish sort of woman," a musician remembered. "She was good-hearted and big-hearted, and she liked to juice, and she liked to sing her blues slow." Another blues singer spoke a gentle epitaph: "Bessie Smith was an old,

old friend and everybody loved her, which was why they was so shocked when she died in that accident. Of course she *did* have enemies. Who don't? She was a very high-tempered person, and she didn't take anything from anybody. But she was a good girl, on the whole." They buried her in Philadelphia.

Though it was generally believed that Bessie left no descendants, Chris Albertson, in his 1972 biography *Bessie,* revealed the existence of Jackie Gee, Jr., an adopted son. Unfortunately he never lived with his mother very much, and though she loved him she could not have been very much of an influence on him. But for Bessie the musician there was never an end to influence. She made about 180 records and that one movie. Some of her songs were poetry, some of them no more than popular tunes of the twenties. But her musical genius, echoes of her remarkable style, remained in the music of those who came after her, even when they made up new ways to sing.

3
Mahalia Jackson

Mahalia Jackson was a churchwoman all her life. She sang at Madison Square Garden and in Carnegie Hall, in European concert halls and on radio and television, but she never sang except in praise of God. Mahalia was a gospel singer, a bearer of the Christian message. Though she wasn't a blues singer and never considered herself one, her story belongs with those of Ma Rainey and Bessie Smith because gospel, blues, and jazz are all interrelated aspects of African American music. It would be impossible to consider one without the others. In African culture there had been no division of life into religious and secular moments—any event of significance was an occasion for "praise" songs: a child's tooth falling out, the onset of puberty, the arrival of visitors, the desire for a traveler's safe return. Musically, this tradition continued in America. Just as spirituals influenced blues and jazz, so blues and jazz influenced gospel music. Mahalia went to church, but she also went to hear Bessie. She was a Baptist Protestant Christian American, celebrating her religion in a way that carried on an African spiritual tradition.

Africans were not offered Christianity at the beginning of their sojourn in America. Only "savages" could be slaves, the churches reasoned, for if you promoted them to Christian brotherhood you could no longer justify enslaving them! But during the seventeenth and early eighteenth century the consciences of white American Christians nagged. The Quakers took the lead, followed by Methodists and Baptists, and by mid-eighteenth century the Christian standpoint had been completely reversed. Slavery, the churches now contended, was a convenient way of transporting "savages" to the "civilized" world in order to save their souls. This done, churchmen undoubtedly figured their converts would sing and pray in the usual manner. But they didn't. Black people invited to church would invariably stomp or clap or wail, and since this just wasn't considered part of a Christian service they were promptly invited out. Not prevented from forming their own church congregations, they altered the given rituals and intermingled these with their own remembered customs—baptism in black churches, for instance, is partly a ritual cleansing from the Dahomey culture in Africa.

In African music, rhythm and timbre (the characteristic "sound" of an instrument or voice) were considered more important than melody and harmony. Music in black Christian churches was therefore not stripped of rhythm to make it "holy"; on the contrary, a great deal of energy and sound was put into religious celebrations. Early spirituals, like the blues that came later, combined some elements of western music and some of African, but the rhythmic emphasis was still clear. Mahalia sometimes complained that white people didn't clap properly: "First you've got to get the rhythm until, through the music, you have the freedom to interpret it." At concerts she would tease: "That's enough darlins. I know you're enjoying yourself, but you just ain't clapping right. If you don't stop, I'm gonna sing something slow."

Whether they clapped or not, white people were definitely attracted to the black Christian service. White revivalist ("gimme that old-time religion") churches began to copy it in the late 1700s, and more than one, instead of converting the Africans to a Christian ritual, ended up converting itself to an African ritual.

The playing of musical instruments and dancing as well as singing had all been part of African praise celebrations. Christianity as given to the slaves left little room for exuberance; religion was supposed to be a serious and solemn affair. By the nineteenth century, however, black Christian congregations had interpreted the Bible to maintain their own ideas of religious experience. For example, though dancing was not permitted, it is defined in the Bible as "crossing of feet." So, since dancing was important to praise celebrations, the "shuffle" was developed. Shuffling permitted movement that was not considered a transgression. It may not have been as satisfying as dancing, but it beat sitting still.

This description of a "ring shout" is from 1867:

> *The benches are pushed back to the wall when the formal meeting is over, and old and young, men and women . . . all stand up in the middle of the floor, and when the "sperchil" is struck up, begin first walking and by-and-by shuffling round, one after the other, in a ring. The foot is hardly taken from the floor, and the progression is mainly due to a jerking, hitching motion which agitates the entire shoulder and soon brings out streams of perspiration. Sometimes they dance silently, sometimes, as they shuffle, they sing the chorus of the spiri-*

> *tual, and sometimes the song itself is also sung by the*
> *dancers. But more frequently a band, composed of some*
> *of the best singers and of tired shouters, stand at the*
> *side of the room to "base" the others, singing the body*
> *of the song and clapping their hands together or on*
> *their knee.*

There were of course those who pressed for less enthusiasm and more "respectability," and their demands persisted even up to Mahalia's day. To one preacher's criticism Mahalia replied, as she noted in her autobiography:

> *I told him I had been reading the Bible every day most*
> *of my life and there was a Psalm that said: "Oh, clap*
> *your hands, all ye people! Shout unto the Lord with the*
> *voice of the trumpet!"*
>   *How can you sing prayerfully of heaven and earth and*
> *all God's wonders without using your hands?*
>   *I want my hands . . . my feet . . . my whole body to say*
> *all that is in me. I say, "Don't let the devil steal the beat*
> *from the Lord! The Lord doesn't like us to act dead. If*
> *you feel it, tap your feet a little—dance to the glory of*
> *the Lord!*

Whether for dancing or for political meetings, church had been the only place slaves were permitted to assemble without fear of reprisal. After emancipation and into the twentieth century the church continued to function as a strong support for black family and communal life, especially in the South. Mahalia was born in New Orleans in 1911, and she described her family's Mount Moriah Baptist Church as a place with "lots going on for children to watch." There were services every evening and silent movies on Saturday night; church was a place where she went often just to play. True, a church member's life was open to scrutiny; saints and sinners alike came under the eye of the elders. But along with this control there was also the underlying assurance of community care.

Brought up by her strict Aunt Duke (Mahalia Paul) after her mother's death, little "Halie" from age five on had to "toe the line," as she described it, or look for the cat-o'-nine-tails. Aunt Duke wasn't much for play; she believed "in the church and hard work and no frills." Mahalia had one dress and no shoes, and no toys. She made her own dolls of rags, with braided grass for hair. She scrubbed floors, made mattresses of moss and corn shucks, collected driftwood from the Mississippi and fallen coal from the railroad yards. From the time she was seven, before going to school, Mahalia went with her twelve-year-old Aunt Bessie to white people's homes to dress their children and do the dishes, returning in the afternoon to work some more. The pay was two dollars a week for both. But the hard work—perhaps not as much *hard* as *real*—was balanced by the security of Mahalia's position as a child in a family that was not only large and mutually supporting, but aware of its own history and determined to make something of life in America. Her eldest uncle had brought his many brothers and sisters one by one down to New Orleans from the sharecropping plantation where their great-grandparents, grandparents, and parents had been slaves. And even though Aunt Duke was heavy on discipline and light on affection, there was kind Uncle Emanuel Paul, with whom Mahalia gardened in the mornings, and her father who held her on his lap and called her his "chocolate drop." She used to visit him in the evenings where he worked as a barber and on Saturdays, when he would

A camp meeting around 1870.

give her money to take to Aunt Duke for the care of her brother Peter and herself.

As Ma's and Bessie's had been, Mahalia's talent also was noticeable early. From the time she was quite small she had been allowed to sing in the church choir. Cousins on her father's side of the family were show people, traveling with Ma Rainey, and when they heard Mahalia sing they asked to take her along. But Aunt Duke would have none of it, even though the opportunity would have meant, as it had for Bessie, a stab at fame and fortune. Mahalia always admired her aunt's strength in refusing, especially because they were so poor. "And she didn't have a dime when she said no to them either. It's easy to be independent when you've got money. But to be independent when you haven't got a thing—that's the Lord's test."

So Mahalia stayed at home and never knew the tent show life or the T.O.B.A. Still, music was available everywhere in New Orleans then—the showboats on the Mississippi had music, there were the city's famous brass marching bands, and jazz bands sometimes played "cutting contests" in the streets.

> *Down the street, in an old sideboard wagon, would come the jazz band from one ballroom. And up the street, in another sideboard wagon, would come the band from another ballroom, which had announced a dance for the same night at the same price. And those musicians played for all their worth, because the band that pleased the crowd more would be the one the whole crowd would go to hear, and dance to, at its ballroom later that night.*

> *Bands in those days fighting all the time. One band get a job in the Love and Charity Hall, another band move right over there and play better through the windows. During Mardi Gras and parades, bands got taken around in wagons, and they'd back them, tailgate to tailgate, and play each other down.*

Mahalia heard ragtime, and jazz—and the blues. By the time she was in her teens there were phonographs and records, too, and when Aunt Duke was out Mahalia listened over and over to the Bessie Smith records her cousin Fred ("Chafalaye") had bought. Handsome and charming, nicknamed after the river near where he was born, Chafalaye preferred high life to church life and knew the New Orleans of four miles away, the legendary Storyville with its cafés and cabarets and "sporting houses." (The Navy closed Storyville in 1917, and many of the musicians left for points north—St. Louis, Kansas City, Chicago.) Mahalia loved her dashing cousin and admired his defiance of Aunt Duke: "He laughed at her scolding and went his way, and she couldn't do anything about it but love him." Chafalaye, and Bessie's haunting blues, were Mahalia's inspiration, though she never carried out her youthful dreams:

> *I don't sing the blues myself—not since those days when I was a child. I don't ever take any nightclub engagements. But you've got to know what the blues meant to us then to understand properly about them. The Negroes all over the South kept those blues playing to give us relief from our burdens and to give us courage to go on and maybe go away.*

> *I remember when I used to listen to Bessie Smith sing "I Hate to See That Evening Sun Go Down," I'd fix my mouth and try to make my tones come out just like hers. And I'd whisper to myself that someday the sun was going to shine down on me way up North in Chicago or Kansas City or one of those other faraway places.*

But it wasn't easy for a girl to break away. Mahalia watched enviously when the other kids in her neighborhood went to the dance hall and held hands on the levee. She quit school after eighth grade to work as a laundress, washing and ironing sometimes for ten hours at a stretch, trying to figure out what to do with her life. Again, as with Bessie, there were not that many choices. Though Mahalia had been brought up to shun the entertainment world where Chafalaye was known, it was tempting as well as frightening, and it would have been something to do. But then Chafalaye died. When Mahalia finally left, despite Aunt Duke's fear that she would fall into a life of sin, it was to go to Chicago to become a nurse. At least that was a "respectable" occupation.

When Mahalia arrived in the North in 1928, Chicago's South Side was a marvel to a country girl:

> *Never before had Negroes lived so well or had so much money to spend. I'll never forget what a joy it was to see them driving up and down Southern Parkway and Michigan Boulevard in big, shiny touring cars and strolling in the evening, laughing and talking and calling out happily to each other. The men wore cream-colored spats and derbies and carried walking sticks. Their women had fur coats and led little dogs on leashes. Many of the houses on Michigan Avenue were mansions and the people that lived there had diamonds and silks and drove Rolls-Royces. They could easily afford them because some Negroes had become millionaires.*

But Mahalia's family was less than rich, and when one of the aunts with whom she was staying took sick Mahalia found herself back at the washtubs, her nursing studies put off indefinitely. She had to travel to work in the bitter Chicago morning: "The cold and the noise seemed to beat on me and the big buildings made me feel as if I'd come to live in a penitentiary." But as it always had been when she felt lonely or misplaced, the church was there to comfort; it provided not only friendship but a sense of purpose, a reality that went beyond the washtub and the ironing board. Mahalia joined the Greater Salem Baptist Church. She sang in the choir and went to socials and picnics and soon had made a life for herself in the cold city. Her homesickness gone, it was fifteen years before she returned to New Orleans to visit.

But the good times Mahalia found in 1928 lasted only for

another year, and then, in her words, when the Depression hit, "it was as if somebody had pulled a switch and everything had stopped running." Without homes or jobs, their savings gone behind the locked doors of banks, black people, especially recent "immigrants," were hard pressed to stay alive. The underworld was one way. There were also "rent parties," where the price of admission included supper and music; the earnings kept the roof over the owner's head and kept a few musicians from going under. Churches were in the same predicament. Ministers who only a year before had watched their congregations drive up to the door in fancy cars now scraped to pay for heat and lights and to keep their buildings from being repossessed. Churches too gave rent parties, only they were called suppers and socials, and the music played wasn't blues but spirituals and other songs of inspiration. Mahalia sang at Greater Salem with the minister's children. They called their group the Johnson Gospel Singers. With the inspiration of piano player Prince Johnson, who arranged their music and whom Mahalia called "the first gospel piano player in Chicago" (he played a "distinctive boogie-woogie piano"), they "improved on the music and strayed from the score" and soon had made a name for themselves. After a while they were singing not only at their home church but all around Chicago and out of town at various Baptist conventions, as interest in "gospel music" increased.

Not that religious music had gone unnoticed before then. Though spirituals influenced the development of blues, they had not disappeared or given way entirely to the "devil music." During the twenties, record companies had been quick to take advantage of the popularity of preachers; recorded sermons sold almost as well as recordings of the blues. In addition to sermons there were records by unaccompanied quartets and larger groups like the Fisk Jubilee Singers, and some by evangelist preachers who played an instrument, usually a guitar. A few of the latter were blues singers recording under pseudonyms. Blind Lemon Jefferson, one of the most popular of the country blues singers, assumed the name Deacon L. J. Bates for his religious numbers. The Reverend F. W. McGee played the piano and sometimes added a cornet, guitar, and drums. The financial plight of the recording industry during the Depression left not only blues singers but singers of religious music out of work. Without the opportunity to make records, they took to the road, and when Mahalia began singing professionally she entered a field where there was already a sizeable audience and other professionals to encounter—"fish and bread" singers, as Mahalia called herself, singing for their supper as well as for the Lord.

The popularity of gospel in the North and West during this time was partly due to the same nostalgia that had attracted people to Bessie's country blues. Mahalia explained: "It was the kind of music colored people had left behind them down South and they liked it because it was just like a letter from home." And home, during the Depression especially, was the place where one had had at least a vegetable garden and maybe a pig or chickens.There had been wild greens to gather, and even without money people had somehow been able to eat. Black people in the North were immigrants in a foreign land that was much more hostile to them in the Depression scramble for work; they longed for their lost innocence in the "old country" though they could never dismiss the injustice that went along with it. Gospel music, like the blues, was a spiritual return for those who could not go back, whose land was long since gone and who had to wait out the bad times, inventing a new kind of perseverance to endure the city as they had the country. There had to be some spiritual sustenance and release from pain if a person was going to live through the dehumanizing anonymity of assembly-line factory work, or the drudgery of being a maid. Mahalia once worked packing dates and mentioned that after a week she felt "ready to have them put *me* in a box!" She preferred to work as a maid in between singing tours, even though that meant cleaning thirty-three rooms each day for ten dollars a week.

> *One of these mornings I'm going to lay down my cross*
>   *and get my crown*
> *As soon as my feet strike Zion, I'm going to lay down my*
>   *heavy burden*
> *I'm gonna put on my robes in glory and move on up a*
>   *little higher . . .*

But the gospel life to which Mahalia turned more and more was no easy way either. Though she sometimes earned as much as fifty dollars a week, she traveled from New York to California and did most of her sleeping sitting up on trains. In 1935 she married Isaac "Ike" Hockenhull, a graduate in chem-

istry of Fisk University, who because of the Depression had become a mail carrier in the post office. But their marriage didn't work out. He understandably didn't want her traveling all the time—"a man doesn't want his wife running all over the country, even if it's for the Lord," Mahalia explained. But he also disagreed with her refusal to sing worldly music—she had been invited to by, among others, Louis Armstrong, who had heard her sing in Chicago. Mahalia knew she could have sung blues and jazz but she felt strongly that this was not her destiny. (She had once made a vow never to enter a theater.) And she never thought of the church as a restriction on her musical style. Songs of faith, she felt, gave her as much room to sing as the blues. In her childhood Mahalia had been impressed with the music of the Sanctified Holiness church next door to Aunt Duke's house. Without an organ and with no choir, the whole congregation had made music, playing the drum, cymbal, tambourine, and steel triangle. "We Baptists sang sweet, and we had the long and short meter on beautiful songs like 'Amazing Grace, How Sweet It Sounds,' but when

those Holiness people tore into 'I'm So Glad Jesus Lifted Me Up!' they came out with some real jubilation."

The shift in interest to gospel music during the thirties had as much to do with the music itself as it had to do with a religious revival. Mahalia singing gospel songs was not just Mahalia singing old spirituals instead of blues and jazz. She did sing spirituals, but the new gospel hymns were written music based on the rhythms that had survived in the sanctified churches, and included some of the same musical forms as the blues. One of the earliest and perhaps the most famous of gospel composers was Thomas A. Dorsey, who had recorded with Ma Rainey as "Georgia Tom," before his decision to play only religious music. He and other composers published their music, toured, and made converts everywhere in the thirties. Gospel was only a "going back" insofar as it accomplished the reintroduction to church music of rhythms that had had spiritual significance, a direct emotional effect on the listener. The Holiness people in New Orleans "had a beat, a powerful beat," Mahalia wrote, "a rhythm we held on to from slavery days, and their music was so strong and expressive it used to bring the tears to my eyes." Resistance to this music came from those who still insisted the black Christian service be a carbon copy of white Protestantism, that all the rest was to be reserved for secular music: "They didn't like the hand-clapping and the stomping and they said we were bringing jazz into the church and it wasn't dignified."

> *I'm going to walk in Jerusalem—*
> *Talk in Jerusalem—*
> *Shout in Jerusalem—*
> *Pray in Jerusalem—*
> *High up in Jerusalem—*
> *When I die!*

People were always after Mahalia to sing differently. In 1932 she took a lesson from a certain Professor DuBois who told her to stop shouting and slow down the tempo, because the way she sang white people would never understand her and she wouldn't be "a credit to the Negro race." Mahalia was baffled: "I felt all mixed up. How could I sing songs for white people to understand when I was colored myself? It didn't seem to make any sense. It was a battle within me to sing a song in a formal way. I felt it was too polished and I didn't feel good about it." That, for four dollars, was Mahalia's first and last singing lesson. Thomas Dorsey tried later on to get her to alter her breathing and phrasing but she refused to sing like anyone else. She put blue notes in gospel, she moaned and growled and "shouted" and her style prevailed. She was also known for her habit of "dancing to the glory of the Lord"—skipping, strutting, and hiking up the long gospel robe when she felt like it. "The girl always had a beautiful voice but she was known for her hollering and getting happy and lifting her dress. Mahalia was always the sexiest thing out there." In later years she ceased to prance, especially in front of white audiences (the critics were always impressed with her dignity). But Mahalia was famous for saying things to her congregations like, "Surely out of all these handsome men, I can find me a good husband." She fell on her knees when the song called for it and the spirit moved her; she would sometimes build a song up and up, singing the words over and over to increase their intensity. *Movin' On Up,* the spiritual that came to be known as "her song," often went on for twenty-five minutes. Gospel songs, even the written ones, could lend themselves—as Mahalia interpreted them—to extensive improvisation. Like Bessie, she would slide up or slur down to a note. She would also break up a word into as many syllables as she cared to, or repeat and prolong an ending to make it more effective: "His love is deeper and deeper, yes deeper and deeper, it's deeper! and deeper, Lord! deeper and deeper, Lord! it's deeper than the se-e-e-e-a, yeah, oh my lordy, yeah, deeper than the sea, Lord." And the last two words would be a dozen syllables each. When someone asked her how she managed the moans and incredible tones, the answer was, "Child, I don't know how I do it myself." After a while Mahalia had many imitators, but none had her voice or her feeling. The story is told that once, counting her change after a program, she realized suddenly that she could now buy the doll she had always wanted but had never had in New Orleans. She began to sing about it: "Lord, I want to thank you for giving me enough money to buy a doll." Her voice carried into the street and people began to shout as though they were in church. The words she was singing didn't matter; those who listened to her responded because she made the depth of her feeling available to them, drew them into her belief, and took them along.

By the forties gospel music had become an institution in black communities. Storefront churches and white-robed sisters were familiar sights; the sound of the tambourine and the rocking beat of the gospel piano were heard as often as the organ chords of familiar Protestant hymns. Sundays and some evening hours gospel took over local black radio stations. Gospel music was a national affair, but a national *Negro* affair. Like Gertrude Rainey, Mahalia was known on the gospel circuit as Mother; like Ma Rainey, Mahalia sang—"in great big gospel tents and little old rackety-rack store-front churches and in big ballrooms"—entirely for her own people. The segregation by law that existed unchallenged in the South until the Supreme Court decisions of the fifties had its counterpart in the *de facto* segregation of the North. As they had in the twenties, black people worked by day in the white world and went home to their own cities or their own suburbs at night. The recordings that Mahalia made in the forties sold very well, in certain places. Gospel was private, African, Negro, black. And Mahalia, like many other artists famous in the world black people laboriously but quietly carved for themselves during this time, had scarcely any contact with whites at all. The novelist Ralph Ellison called his character the "invisible man." Some years later, a white writer who looked over and was shocked by some of the conditions he found in this black world, called his book *The Other America.*

But in 1950 the jazz critics discovered Mahalia, and not long afterward she sang the first of what came to be regular concerts in Carnegie Hall. Then Europe discovered her—in Paris the police had to keep back the crowd, in Copenhagen children filled her hotel lobby with flowers, in Denmark her record of *Silent Night* became a best-seller. Television followed radio, but she found it difficult because of the time: "I'm used to singing in church till the spirit comes. Here they want everything done in two or three minutes." In 1954 Columbia began to record her, and after a while orchestras, choirs, and harps began to appear in the background. Mahalia invariably was at her best with only Mildred Falls, her accompanist for many years, at the piano.

Through recordings and appearances Mahalia became a celebrity, a star who was known everywhere. She had her own opinions about this. When a newspaperman asked her why she thought white people came to hear her, she answered: "Well, honey, maybe they tried drink and they tried psychoanalysis and now they're going to try to rejoice with me a bit." People did rejoice with Mahalia, but though they sang and clapped and maybe even "felt the spirit" there was still a great deal of work, a lot of convincing to be done. Mahalia was famous and she could have become rich through gospel, but she never "went commercial"; she never sang in nightclubs, though once she was offered $10,000 a week to do so. She turned instead to the civil rights movement, singing benefits wherever she could for the bus boycotts, the student sit-ins, for Martin Luther King's Southern Christian Leadership Conference. She was an admirer of President Kennedy and he of her—she sang for his inauguration in 1961. But the murders of Dr. King and the Kennedys, the violence of the sixties, confused and saddened her. Shots were fired through the windows of the house she had bought in a white suburb in Chicago. And after the joy she had felt at the March on Washington in 1963, with everyone together for a better world, it didn't seem that the neighbors should move away but they did. Mahalia felt that she "had lived to see another time," and she referred to the sixties as "the worst times since the days of slavery for relations between white and black."

Nevertheless she did not cease to believe in nonviolence, or in Christianity. When asked how she managed to carry on she replied: "There can be no turning away. There's a right to feel doubtful and despondent about things but that is the time when you can't let your spirit and determination weaken." Mahalia felt also that the church had not outlived its usefulness, that it could continue to be a source of strength for people as it had in the past. She believed it might be, as it had been for her, a place to find friendship, help, consolation, and the mutual support of the community, a group that might sing together to lift up and maintain its collective spirit.

The later sixties were a time of mixed blessings for Mahalia. Upset by race relations and world conditions, she turned again to church work. She broadcast on local radio, raising funds for Greater Salem: "Come on over and let Halie cook you her fine

New Orleans gumbo." In 1965 she married Sigmund Gal-
loway, a builder who was also a musician, and for a time was
very happy. (They were divorced not long after, but later
remarried.) Mahalia banished her image as a solid, solemn,
dignified old lady by skipping and strutting both on television
and at the Newport Jazz Festival. When a television interviewer asked her how she felt about getting old, her reply was
typically Mahalian: "I don't feel nothing—I am old, but I look
pretty good for an old girl, don't I?"

Mahalia believed that gospel was great American music. She
wasn't sure she liked "pop gospel" (though her critics accused
her of singing it herself) or "soul music," which she consid-

ered an exploitation. But she was realistic: "It was bound to be picked up and used just the way the white people have used other music that came out of the black people's world, like jazz and the blues." She also knew that interest in gospel would pass, like all other fashions in music, and that what she called "real gospel music" would remain because its strength lay in its power to reach "the heart and human spirit."

Mahalia lived to see and be affected by the growing insistence in most African American communities that their culture is valuable, an identity to be preserved. She astonished a Harlem audience by putting down ministers who had been "too scared" to bring Martin Luther King to Chicago, leaving the job to her, a woman. Of the old songs, she explained: "They're brand new to me. Man, I was down South. You should hear those choirs in South Carolina and Georgia. They sing those hymns, and tears run from my eyes. I just want to jump up and shout. Looks like I find myself when I hear them. We lose something up North, ain't no need fooling ourselves. But when I hear those folks, I sort of get refilled, get what I had when I was a child."

Mahalia had to come a long way to get back home, but she couldn't stay around too long to enjoy it. She died at the end of January 1972, of a heart ailment that had troubled her on and off during her later years, but which she had refused to allow to interfere with her work, with the hundreds of concerts she sang each year. Forty thousand people came to say good-bye to her at Greater Salem before she was taken home to be buried near New Orleans. At a memorial service in Chicago's biggest theater, the Reverend C. L. Franklin preached that Mahalia "had lived in a house she tried to repair," and his daughter Aretha sang *Precious Lord Take My Hand,* over and over till the walls echoed with it. Would Mahalia have objected to the theater? Perhaps not, despite her early vow, for by the end of her life she had sung in many places where the usual fare was entertainment. But it never mattered just where she sang, for she took the church with her. As someone once put it, "she could turn a tavern into a temple if she chose to."

Mahalia had always been people, as her people say, and if she was able to turn taverns into temples, so were they. Under the worst possible slum conditions, out of unheated stores and abandoned churches and synagogues they made holy places, where they could sing and praise and feel a spirit they knew was meant to be. If you didn't believe, the old people would tell you, you were merely mistaken. Church was a place where a person was no longer the maid or the handyman with only a first name, but a place where black men and women stood apart in their natural dignity, to save and nourish that precious possession, the soul. Given little else they kept that, and looked for a time when others would come to them for help in finding their own.

Precious Lord, take my hand,
Lead me on, let me stand
I am tired, I am weak, I am worn.
Through the storm, through the night
Lead me on to the light
Take my hand, precious Lord, lead me on.

When my way grows drear
Precious Lord linger near
When my life is almost gone
At the river, Lord I'll stand
Guide my feet, hold my hand
Take my hand, precious Lord,
*   and lead me home.*

4

Billie Holiday

One day we were so hungry we could barely breathe. I started out the door. It was cold as all-hell and I walked from 145th to 133rd . . . going in every joint trying to find work. . . . I stopped in the Log Cabin Club run by Jerry Preston . . . told him I was a dancer. He said to dance. I tried it. He said I stunk. I told him I could sing. He said sing. Over in the corner was an old guy play-ing the piano. He struck Trav'lin' *and I sang. The cus-tomers stopped drinking. They turned around and watched. The pianist . . . swung into* Body and Soul. *Jeez, you should have seen those people—all of them started crying. Preston came over, shook his head and said, "Kid, you win."*

Billie Holiday was not quite seventeen then; it was 1932. Before she was done singing in the summer of 1959 many more people had cried over her *Trav'lin' All Alone* and *Body and Soul.* These were popular songs, as were most numbers she sang, and other people recorded and performed them. But Billie transformed them. She was a jazz singer; she put the blues inside and made each song her own. She thought of her voice as an instrument: "I don't think I'm singing," she explained. "I feel like I'm playing a horn. . . . What comes out is what I feel."

A lot of different feelings came out of Billie's horn—she sang for over twenty-five years, in the United States and Europe as well. She could be gentle, funny, sarcastic, heart-breaking. Her honesty about feeling was what made people cry; she found it hard to lie. Astonished critics exclaimed: "She appears to mean every word she is singing," and "You believed every word she sang." There were some words about which Billie was especially believable. People told her no one sang "hunger" like she did, or "love." She sang what she knew, a first rule in playing jazz as Charlie Parker explained it: "Music is your own experience, your thoughts, your wisdom. If you don't live it, it won't come out of your horn." Billie said simply, "You just feel it, and when you sing it other people can feel something too."

Born Eleanora Fagan, called Billie Holiday and titled Lady Day—she was a beautiful woman, this First Lady of jazz. Much of her life was a sad song and a bitter story, and heroin as well as hunger and love overwhelmed her finally when she was only forty-four. The recordings she left still tell about it. Some people can let her sing on and on while they listen: "Lady Day has suffered so much she carries it all for you," says a young man in an English novel. But for others the blues, meant for response, carry the listener as well. Either you go with Billie or let her go, and sometimes you have to choose, as Amiri Baraka (LeRoi Jones) has written:

*At the point where what she did left singing, you were on
your own. At the point where what she was was in her
voice, you listen and make your own promises. More
than I have felt to say she says always. . . .*
Sometimes you are afraid to listen to this lady.

But Billie's difficult life, even as the source of her feeling,
should never obscure her musical genius. More than anything
else, like Bessie whom she admired, Billie was a great artist.

By 1932 even the hard life of an artist looked better than
other ways she had tried to take care of herself. Billie was a
city girl, raised in Baltimore. Her mother, Sadie Fagan, was
nineteen when Billie was born and her father, Clarence Holiday, only seventeen. They never married. World War I took
Clarence overseas, and after that his musical ambitions often
took him on the road. He did give Billie her nickname, though.
Because she was a tomboy he called her Bill, which she
stretched to Billie after Billie Dove, her favorite movie star.
She may have been tough but she was a tough *girl.*

To Sadie's respectable family, Billie was an unwanted child
who was sure to inherit her mother's "badness." They certainly
did their best to make her angry. In an autobiography written for
her many years later, Billie described a childhood that was not
only hard but brief and often painful. Her cousin Ida ruled the
household and, among other things, beat Billie when her own
son Henry wet the bed. For a while the family lived with their
elderly great-grandmother, whom Billie loved, and who, during
slavery, had borne sixteen children to her owner. "We used to
talk about life," Billie remembered. "And she used to tell me
how it felt to be a slave, to be owned body and soul. . . . She
couldn't read or write, but she knew the Bible . . . and she was
always ready to tell me a story from the Scriptures." One night

the old lady persuaded Billie to let her lie down to sleep (Billie didn't know that because of an illness she wasn't supposed to). She died later, her arm locked around Billie's neck. Afterward, Billie told her biographer, Ida only had something else to beat her for.

For a while at some point, it looked as if the Fagans' situation might change. Sadie married a longshoreman named Phil Gough, and they lived in a nice house. But after three years, Phil Gough disappeared, leaving them to struggle—Sadie for the rent, Billie for direction.

A truant at ten, she was sent as "a minor without proper care and guardianship" to a home for wayward girls. Billie later told terrible tales of this place, where most of the girls were much older, rules were strict, and punishment severe. At the home each girl exchanged her clothes for a uniform and was given a new name—a new, "better" self. If disobedient, she was made to wear a ragged red dress; the others were not permitted to speak to or go near her. During her stay, Billie said, one girl being punished like this had pushed herself higher and higher on a swing until it broke and she flew, screaming, to her death. The night Billie was made to wear the red dress she was locked in a room with the body of another girl who had died. "It's terrible what something like this does to you," she said in her autobiography. "It takes years and years to get over it; it haunts you and haunts you."

Eventually, her mother and grandfather found a lawyer to get her out, and Billie came home to live with Sadie and a man named Wee Wee Hill. She must have been, if not happy, at least relieved, because Hill later remembered her singing around the house. But then he and Sadie went North to work. Billie was left in the well-intentioned but inadequate care of his bedridden mother, in a busy home where boarders and other Hill relatives lived.

Baltimore in the twenties had a lively nightlife that included "good time houses," where attractive girls like Billie were welcome. People went to these houses to talk, drink, and dance, and sometimes to rent rooms—and girls—for sex. Music, some recorded, some live, was a big part of the party. In Baltimore, as in most cities where black people lived in large numbers, there were also jazz clubs and "after hours" places where musicians gathered to play to each other. Billie's father Clarence was now a well-known guitarist. As Mahalia had her cousin Chafalaye, Billie had Clarence to look to for an alternative. In Billie's case, with Sadie up North and no one to stop her, she began to skip school by day and hang out at night to listen to music. At twelve, virtually on her own, she was big

Harlem in the early thirties.

for her age, plump, pretty, and desirable, and before long she was working in a good time house as a prostitute.

A home—"nice" or not—is a house where you feel wanted, and where you can find a life. Billie was popular. Older women befriended her. She kept singing; she was *asked* to sing. She sat in with other young, up-and-coming jazz musicians, and became *part* of the music. In a sense, because jazz is improvised, in Baltimore she trained for the rest of her artistic life. She listened not only to locals like Clarence (who also sang sometimes), but to others who came to town to play, and to recordings, especially by her favorites, Louis Armstrong and Bessie Smith. *Where* she heard music was far less important than *what* she heard. As she said, "If I'd heard Louis and Bessie at a Girl Scout jamboree, I'd have loved them just the same."

At fifteen Billie left Baltimore to join Sadie in Harlem. Reunited with her mother, she went looking for her father, who had also come to New York. Clarence, playing then with the famous Fletcher Henderson Orchestra, introduced Billie to the New York music scene. (Although he didn't appreciate her calling him Daddy in front of his lady friends, especially when she was asking him for money.) As she had in Baltimore, Billie jammed with the best musicians, and eventually became a regular, working for tips, in Harlem's small clubs. Tips, though sometimes generous, are hardly predictable. The Log Cabin debut Billie described was probably not really the first time she'd sung professionally, but these details are less important than the fact that by 1932, at seventeen, despite the presence of her parents, Billie knew that survival was up to her. She would later make that feeling famous in a song called "God Bless the Child (that's got his own)." But in 1932 she asked the pianist to play *Trav'lin' All Alone* because "that came closer than anything to the way I felt."

I'm so weary and all alone
Feet are tired like heavy stone,
Trav'lin', trav'lin', all alone.

Who will see and who will care
Bout this load that I must bear,
Trav'lin', trav'lin', all alone.

Jerry Preston hired Billie for eighteen dollars a week. She sang every night from midnight to 3 A.M., and by 1933 many people had come to hear her. She acquired an agent and began to work at various clubs; and—for John Hammond, who had just made Bessie Smith's last recording—she made her first record and was paid thirty-five dollars for the effort. People expected a lot for thirty-five dollars in those days. The owner of an employment agency reported receiving a request for "a 'nice colored woman' who could cook and typewrite for thirty-five dollars a month."

Many of those who listened to Billie would try to pin down her style. When critics asked how she did it she was quite specific: Bessie Smith and Louis Armstrong were her only influences—she had always aimed for "Bessie's big sound and Pops' feeling." But no one could really *describe* her singing. A disc jockey told the manager of the Apollo Theater, "It ain't the blues. I don't know what it is, but you got to hear her." When he did he hired her, and Billie sang at the Apollo, which has always been considered an achievement. Her first performance was at 10 A.M., she had been up all the night before singing at a club, and she was so scared she was shaking. Later she remembered the audience: "They were wide awake early in the morning. They didn't ask me what my style was, who I was, how I had evolved, where I'd come from, who influenced me, or anything. They just broke the house up."

But people liking your music didn't always mean you'd eat. What little money there was around was spread so thin it amounted to nothing. Danny Barker remembered how it was:

> *The depression for musicians in New York—man, it was a bitch! I was working, I remember, in the Lenox Club, and there was a ten-piece band, eight chorus girls, four waiters, two bartenders, two managers, a doorman, a porter, and a "whiskey man."*
>
> *The hours were like from ten in the evening to five in the morning. . . . At the end of the night they would pull a table into the middle of the floor and spill out the receipts of the night on the table and give everybody an equal share. Some mornings we'd make seventy-five cents, other mornings we'd get twenty-five. Everybody cooperated, because there was nowhere else to go and, in fact, nobody had nothin'.*

Even Billie's earnings didn't go far. To help out, Sadie sold fried chicken dinners at their apartment, but she was not the world's best businesswoman—she had a tendency to forget the charges. Sadie liked people and had faith in them. Despite her early neglect of Billie, she seems to have been a good person, and a good mother after Billie came to New York. Billie adored her and never really minded Sadie's overgenerosity. She described their home as "a boardinghouse for broke musicians, soup kitchen for anyone with a hard-luck story, community center, and after-after-hours joint. . . . All you had to do was tell Mom you were a musician and give her a little story and she'd give you everything in the house that wasn't nailed down."

Of the many fine musicians in New York at that time, Billie especially liked to sing with saxophonist Lester Young: "I used to love to have him come around and blow pretty solos behind me." It was Lester who gave Billie her title. People had been calling her "Lady" ever since at one club she had refused to take customers' tips off the tables without using her hands. (Without hands you've got only elbows and knees and have to expose more than you would if you didn't need the money. This was a well-established custom. Some of the blues singers of the twenties had also refused—Bessie for one.) Billie tried—she had even bought fancy underwear for the purpose—but she kept messing up. Finally one man called her a "punk kid" because she kept dropping the twenty-dollar bill he had set out for her. Afterwards he had a change of heart and put the money in her hand. From then on Billie decided that anyone who wanted to give her a tip could just hand it over. Other women at the club would taunt: "Look at her, she thinks she's a lady." So Lady she was, and when Lester added the "day" out of Holiday, Billie became Lady Day. In return she titled Lester the President, or Pres, because she thought he was "the world's greatest." "Lester sings with his horn," Billie said. "You listen to him and can almost hear the words." Lester convinced Lady Day and Sadie, whom he had named the Duchess, that life was dangerous for a young man alone, even the President. So they gave him the room off the airshaft. "It was wonderful having a gentleman around the house," Billie recalled. "We were the Royal Family of Harlem."

Earning a living was still so uncertain in New York that when Billie was offered fourteen dollars a day to tour with Count Basie's band, she accepted. Lester would be along to look out for her, and she thought traveling would be fun. But it turned out to be less romantic than she'd anticipated. They traveled everywhere by bus, sometimes covering five or six hundred miles between engagements. The fourteen dollars was barely enough to pay for necessities and for hotel rooms, where instead of sleeping they "took a long look at the bed." Mostly they slept on the bus—or tried to. They played the South and the Midwest—for black audiences and white. They didn't have time to rehearse and they didn't always have the proper horns or equipment. It was something like the T.O.B.A. but modernized—the railroad had been replaced by a Blue Goose bus. Most jazz musicians were city people like Billie; many were northerners. The South was a different place still. As the minstrels had discovered a century before, musicians were not always welcome. Earl "Fatha" Hines, the pianist, said that going South was "an invasion" for them:

> *Things happened all the time. They made us walk in the street off the sidewalk in Fort Lauderdale, and at a white dance in Valdosta, Georgia, some hecklers in the crowd turned off the lights and exploded a bomb under the bandstand. . . . Sometimes when we came into a town that had a bad reputation the driver would tell us—and here we were in our own chartered bus—to move to the back of the bus just to make it look all right and not get anyone riled up.*

With only the scenery out the window and each other for company, they enjoyed themselves when they could:

> *We were always seeing new territory, new beauty. In those days the country was a lot more open and sometimes we'd run into another band and just park the buses by the road and get out and play baseball in a field.*

. . . and how they could:

> *There was always a little tonk game [cards] on the bus*
> *at night. The boys put something for a table across the*
> *aisle and sat on Coke boxes and hung a light from the*
> *luggage rack on a coat hanger. . . . They played most of*
> *the night, and it was amusing and something to keep you*
> *interested if you couldn't sleep.*

Billie once spent twelve hours on her knees throwing dice, on the floor of the bus from West Virginia to New York—and won $1,000 to take home to her mother.

Count Basie was originally from the New York area. Stranded in Kansas City in the late twenties, he had found musicians who shared his sympathies and he had stayed on. What the Basie group brought with them out of their home was a skill they had been perfecting long before they took to the road. A lot of music had been played in Kansas City during the early thirties; many people went there just to be part of what was going on. Before Billie sang with Count Basie her group experience had been at jam sessions, or with studio orchestras that depended on written out "arrangements" to keep each band member carefully playing his part in place. The Basie band's style of group improvisation appealed to her because it avoided the kind of copying which she knew could lead to a lack of feeling. Though they did use arrangements, these were "edited" by Basie; solos were improvised and a tune rarely played the same way twice. Billie remembered later how the sixteen of them worked up arrangements of pop songs for her: "The cats would come in, somebody would hum a tune. Then someone else would play it over on the piano once or twice. Then someone would set up a riff [rhythmic pattern], a ba-deep, a ba-dop. Then Daddy Basie would two-finger it a little. And then things would start to happen." The band, according to Billie, knew about a hundred songs without music and from memory. Those among them who did read music, as she pointed out, "didn't want to

Billie with Vic Dickenson and Adolphus "Doc" Cheatham.

be bothered anyway." But this deceptively casual approach was after all an approach by people who *could* do it. They knew their instruments, they knew music, and they knew each other:

> *We'd get off a bus after a five-hundred-mile trip, go into the [recording] studio with no music, nothing to eat but coffee and sandwiches. . . .*
>
> *I'd say, "What'll we do, a two-bar or four-bar intro?"*
>
> *Somebody'd say make it four and a chorus—one, one and a half.*
>
> *Then I'd say, "You play behind me the first eight, Lester," and then Harry Edison would come in or Buck Clayton and take the next eight bars. "Jo, you just brush and don't hit the cymbals too much." . . . If we were one side short on a date, someone would say, "Try the blues in A flat," and tell me, "Go as far as you can go, honey."*

Musicians were especially impressed with Billie's sense of time. Bobby Tucker, who played piano for her, explained:

> *One thing about Lady, she was the easiest singer I ever played for. You know, with most singers you have to guide 'em and carry 'em along—they're either layin' back or else runnin' away from you. But not Billie Holiday. Man, it was a thrill to play for her. She had the greatest conception of a beat I ever heard. It just didn't matter what kind of a song she was singin'. She could sing the fastest tune in the world or else something that was like a dirge, but you could take a metronome and she'd be right there. Hell! With Lady you could relax*

*while you were playin' for her. You could damn near for-
get the tune.*

Though Billie never "forgot" her tunes, she always altered
them. "I hate straight singing," she said. "I have to change a
tune to my own way of doing it." Her ways were surprising
and effective, almost always making more of a tune than its
composer had. For popular songs Billie had a light but sharp
sarcasm, "a mixture of clarity and caricature," someone called
it, as in "Ooo-oo-oo / What a lil moonlight can do-oo-oo."
When she felt that a song was worthy of serious attention she
treated it with great care, emphasizing the beauty she found
there. When it came to the blues, she simply sang, straight out,
in her clear, controlled voice, and let the feeling come through.
The timbre or tone of her voice varied. At the bottom of the
scale she would be hoarse, sometimes growly like a saxophone; higher up she'd sound like an oboe; at the top she could
ring like a bell.

Billie was someone to look at too, and she was careful about
her appearance because she believed it important. That was an
elegant time—sophisticated women were supposed to be
glamorous—and despite having traveled on a bus for days,
Billie liked to appear onstage in a beautiful gown with her hair
done and her makeup just so. She tended to be round rather
than slender, and when she sang she'd tilt her head back a little
and snap her fingers softly. People writing about the way she
looked then were often vague—it was the strange and haunting quality of her voice that captured them. It was through her
voice that she established her personality. As an old friend
pointed out, that voice was "really Lady," for singing was the
only way she could show her real self.

But Billie found it difficult enough just to be herself without interference. She stayed with Count Basie's band for two years and finally quit when they were playing an extended engagement in Detroit, which was "between race riots then," as she remembered it. Among other things, the manager of the theater insisted that Billie blacken her face so audiences not mistake her light skin for white and get upset about her sitting onstage with sixteen black musicians.

Her next tour, in 1937, was with sixteen white musicians in Artie Shaw's band, and though they looked after her she again couldn't be herself without causing trouble. This time there was even more of it. In the South there were big scenes when Billie wanted to eat; she remembered one musician yelling at a waitress who had refused: "This is Lady Day. Now you feed her!" Sleeping and finding a bathroom presented the same problem and at least one time she was in pain for months because of inadequate medical attention. But Billie preferred the South's clarity ("What's Blackie going to sing?" a Kentucky sheriff asked) to the North's hypocrisy. When at last the band had enough of a reputation to play New York, they appeared at a hotel from which radio broadcasts originated. The hotel refused to let Billie be heard on coast-to-coast radio, the biggest deal in those days. But the refusal came slowly. First the management gave her a separate room, then showed her how to come in the back door, and finally cut her off the air.

Artie Shaw's band wasn't any musical milestone for Billie; in fact a *Downbeat* critic suggested that her talents were being wasted: "Artie has a swell group but they don't show off Billie any." By 1939 Billie had decided not to sing with any more dance bands—which is what most of the "swing" bands were—because there were always too many managers telling everyone what to do. The managers were there because jazz—

or what sometimes passed for it—had become big bands, big sound, big business by the late thirties. As far back as the twenties, white musicians had learned to play jazz, some of them well. By the time swing was the thing, they were getting the jobs that paid, at the radio stations and in the recording studios. Black musicians could play together, certainly, but they couldn't make a living. Their own people still had little or no money to pay them, still were hungry and out of work. "Last winter," a newspaper columnist reported in the late thirties, "while men stood idly and starvingly by, two and one-half miles of Harlem's beloved boulevard—Seventh Avenue—was repaved by a crew of all whites." In Harlem the Depression lasted a long time.

So Billie went downtown. At Cafe Society, a new nightclub in Greenwich Village, the management had promised to do away with segregationist policies. Blacks and whites would work together and sit together in the audience. In December 1938 Billie opened the cafe's first show and was very successful. She became a celebrity, though an underpaid one. Her engagement, which lasted more than a year, paid seventy-five dollars a week. But Cafe Society attracted a jazz-loving, integrated crowd, and Billie came to know some of white society's attitudes. She especially resented the assumption that all black-white relationships were of a sexual nature—it was degrading to be accused of having an affair every time she went out for a drink with a friend.

Billie left Cafe Society a star and went next to the place where all the other stars were then—California: Hollywood, Los Angeles, the San Fernando Valley. Many movie people came to listen to her. Bob Hope defended her once when someone heckled her, and Clark Gable fixed her car. Billie had a good time in California; it was very glamorous and added that kind of air to her. She said she came home from Hollywood knowing more about clothes and makeup but still as poor as ever. She had to come all the way back to New York by bus. Traveling cross-country by bus in the 1940s meant one traveled on a series of buses subject to different state laws. No doubt Billie had to ride in the back at least part of the way home. That was the thing about being a black celebrity—one was invariably two people: the star on the stage and the black person who lived in the world. A famous trumpeter told how this conflict made him feel:

> *When I was with Artie Shaw, I went to a place where we were supposed to play a dance and they wouldn't even let me in the place. "This is a white dance," they said, and there was my name right outside, Roy "Little Jazz" Eldridge, and I told them who I was.*
>
> *When I finally did get in, I played that first set, trying to keep from crying.*

*Man, when you're on the stage, you're great, but as
soon as you come off, you're nothing.*

When Billie returned to New York she got a job as an intermission feature at a nightclub on Fifty-second Street, known then as Swing Street, and soon she became one of its main attractions. Working on The Street, she recalled, was like a homecoming every night. Some nights there were as many as five trumpets and five saxophones on the stand all at once. In any of the big bands of the thirties this would not have been remarkable, but Swing Street clubs were small and intimate, most of them having started out as speakeasies during Prohibition.

Though downtown was where the money could be made, Harlem was still where musical decisions were made, at places like Minton's Playhouse and Clarke Monroe's Uptown House. Billie had often worked the Uptown House and naturally she went there to see and jam with her friends. It was around this time that she met Jimmy Monroe (Clarke's younger brother).

He had been around, even to Europe; he was handsome and he was, as Billie said, "a big deal." When they eloped in 1941, Billie was triumphant—Sadie had disapproved of the relationship, claiming he'd never marry her. Jimmy Monroe had good taste and "class," but he too had a "past," and Billie felt that made them equals. He also had a mistress he never gave up, and a drug habit he showed no sign of giving up either, even when Billie found out about it. But she wanted to be with him, and to have a successful marriage. She was now in her late twenties; she wanted to be happy, and she wasn't. She had quarreled with Sadie over Jimmy, and it looked as if she had made a mistake. It was at this time that she began to use heroin. Jimmy gave it to her first, and got it for her when after a while she was hooked. She never had any idea of what a habit would mean until she found herself in Los Angeles, alone because Jimmy had gotten into trouble, faced with the problem of having to provide herself with drugs. Billie said she felt like a baby who was hungry but too helpless to do any-

thing about it but cry, and it didn't help that she knew it was all her own fault.

There was a lot of heroin around musicians in the forties, but even those who eventually died of a habit swore it never did their music any good. Though they may have thought they were playing better, as Charlie Parker explained, they actually weren't. "If you think you need stuff to play music or sing, you're crazy," Billie said. "It can fix you so you can't play nothing or sing nothing." At least some of the addiction can be blamed on the confusion of the times: there was a painful amount of coming and going, as World War II affected everyone's life.

Billie spent those years saying good-bye to lonely soldiers, and to everyone else who was leaving her then. Her marriage was finished. Her father, whose lungs had been damaged during World War I, had caught cold while touring in Texas. Unwilling to risk Jim Crow treatment, he'd waited until he could get to a veterans hospital in Dallas. But by then it was too late, and he died of pneumonia. The Street, too, was disappearing, along with the friendship and the learning atmosphere that had been its attraction. Drugs meant pushers, who preyed on audiences even more than on musicians—a serviceman on leave was an easy mark for hustlers. Club owners deserted Fifty-second Street for Broadway, where everything was much bigger and they could make more money. Billie earned $1,000 a week on Broadway, but most of it went for junk. She was living with trumpeter Joe Guy then, whom she had met when she had first begun to need someone who "could be a big help," as she put it, in getting her drugs. With a thousand a week and a steady supply, Billie was "one of the highest paid slaves around."

It was after her mother died that she began to falter. Perhaps, as one friend suggested, it was Sadie who had held her up all the time: "Her mother fed her well and loved her so. Maybe that's what helped to carry her before. Maybe after she lost her mother, she kind of goofed." She recalled coming home with Billie and Joe Guy from the funeral: "She was telling him over and over again, 'Joe I don't have anybody in the world now except you.' She needed someone to say that to. She felt completely alone."

Billie felt guilty too, thinking she'd worried her mother to an early grave by becoming an addict. In 1946 she entered a hospital that for $2,000 promised complete privacy and medical attention while she kicked her habit. Her mother would have been proud. But there was no Sadie now, to provide the kind of trust and support any ex-addict needs. There were only club owners and managers, all sympathetic and helpful but in the long run having their own attitudes about drug addiction. Soon after Billie had paid all that money she realized that someone had betrayed her confidence, perhaps the hospital—she never knew. But she knew the Narcotics Bureau was after her, waiting for her to make a mistake. An addict was a criminal to be pursued, and an ex-addict was the same. Agents tailed her for a year, from New York to California and points between. It was the United States of America versus Billie Holiday from then on for the rest of her life, a series of *pas de deux* in a long slow dance of death.

In May 1947, Billie was arrested for possession of narcotics. Sick and alone, she signed away her right to a lawyer and no one advised her to do differently, though Joe Guy and another man arrested along with her went free on technicalities. Billie was convinced that no one *could* help her, even if someone had wanted to. Her agent only suggested that it was the best thing that could have happened to her, her New York lawyer refused to come down to Philadelphia for the trial, and she was too wealthy to qualify for legal aid. She was terribly sick and had been given morphine when she appeared in the courtroom. Billie had been promised a hospital cure in return for a plea of guilty; instead she was convicted as a "criminal defendant," a "wrongdoer," and sentenced to a year and a day in the Federal Women's Reformatory at Alderson, West Virginia.

At Alderson, which was segregated, Billie had to endure cold turkey withdrawal. She was further "cured" by performing useful cleaning chores, hauling coal, keeping pigs, and setting tables. She was not allowed to receive any of the letters and gifts that arrived from people all over the world who wanted to remind her that they loved her. She could have used more love and less work, and she also needed to reconsider her addiction with some sort of guidance. But this was not given; as she said later, "With all the doctors, nurses, and equipment, they never get near your insides at what's really eating you." Billie never once sang during the ten months she was in jail. When asked to, her answer was that she was there to be punished, and that was that.

Despite her temporary "cure," Billie's encounter with the law had disastrous results. She held on to her sense of shame, to the idea of herself as a "wrongdoer." "When I die," she said in her book, "they're going to start me off in hell and move me from bad to worse." (Billie, like her mother, was Catholic.) But the worst punishment came in the world to which she returned. She was denied a "cabaret card," the New York police permit that was required for any engagement over four days in a club where liquor was sold. None of the nightclubs where Billie had sung could hire her. Friends tried to help. Ten days after she left Alderson, she gave a successful Carnegie Hall concert (singing thirty-four songs after not having sung for ten months). A Broadway show was organized around her, but though it was well received it closed after three weeks.

And Billie's singing belonged in the intimate atmosphere of a nightclub; she preferred to work in clubs. Her manager could do nothing, since legally she could not work New York.

Illegally was something else again. Billie met a man named John Levy and opened at his Ebony Club; obviously he had his own kind of police permit. Levy worked Billie hard for a while. She made a lot of money, most of which he kept, although he also kept her in minks and Cadillacs with telephones. In 1949, when she decided she had had enough of luxury, he tried to frame her by getting her arrested on a phony dope charge. The fact that John Levy was a liar and a police informer and that Billie Holiday was clean at the time made little difference. It was Billie who had to endure once more the notoriety, the headlines—"Billie Holiday Arrested on Narcotics Charges"—and most of all, people's contempt. She had grown very wary of public acclaim anyway; when crowds showed up at her performances she suspected they'd come to see how high she was.

With the help of friends who made sure she had a very good lawyer, Billie proved her innocence and was acquitted, but it took months, and money. It took her a while to get free of Levy too. She solved the work problem by playing clubs in every major city *except* New York, but she referred to herself as a DP—a "displaced person," the name given to refugees after World War II. As far as New York was concerned, she was Billie Holiday, junkie, and she had been kicked out.

After her involvement with Levy, between out-of-town engagements Billie lived alone in a New York hotel, until she married Louis McKay. She'd first met McKay when she was sixteen, but they had not had an ongoing relationship (as the 1972 movie, *Lady Sings the Blues,* suggests). He is said to have mistreated her. With Louis, Billie toured Europe, where she was greeted with enthusiasm and respect; she in turn was impressed with the European attitude toward jazz.

When Billie played her yearly concerts at the Apollo and at Carnegie Hall everyone came out in full force, either to hear her sing or to contrast her with her past self. Every new record was compared with her early ones, and she was often judged to be imitating herself, to be working with the wrong musicians, the wrong arrangers, etc. Most everyone liked to believe that Billie had been at her best when she sang with Count Basie and the other geniuses of swing. It's hard to disagree, for she was, like all of them, an incredible horn in those days. Billie's later records, usually in a much slower tempo, are a different music. They are the songs of a woman alone and lonely and without much sympathy. No one blows pretty solos behind her like Lester did. Sometimes there are unintelligent voices in the background going "oo-oo-oo" with none of the wit she had on "Ooo-oo-oo what a lil moonlight can doo-oo-oo." Nevertheless, these are the songs of Lady Day too, and if the sorrow sounds a little heavier, it was because she'd been carrying it a while. "I remember when she was happy," Carmen McRae said in 1955. "That was a long time ago."

Billie and Louis both were arrested in 1956. Billie knew by this time that if the Narcotics Bureau wanted to get her it only had to be arranged, the evidence "found" and she could be convicted on her past record. In her autobiography she pleaded that the addict be treated rather than punished. She knew how little good punishment had ever done her. And her stated purpose in revealing all that she considered shameful in her life was to warn young people away from heroin. "If you think dope is for kicks and for thrills, you're out of your mind. . . . The only thing that can happen to you is sooner or later you'll get busted, and once that happens, you'll never live it down. Just look at me."

Billie never was able to stop using heroin completely, though she tried very hard. Some people thought she could have tried harder: "That girl's life . . . was just snapped away from foolishness." But there were others who knew and loved her. Lena Horne and Billie had been friends since Cafe Society days, and

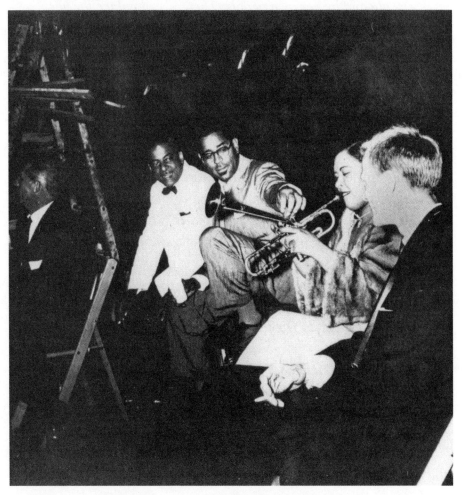

Billie in the mid-fifties with Stan Kenton, Teddy Wilson, Dizzy Gillespie, and Gerry Mulligan.

103

Lena understood how life had been spoiled for her:

> *Billie didn't lecture me—she didn't have to. Her whole*
> *life, the way she sang, made everything very plain. It*
> *was as if she were a living picture there for me to see*
> *something I had not seen clearly before. Her life was so*
> *tragic and so corrupted by other people—by white peo-*
> *ple and by her own people. There was no place for her*
> *to go, except finally, into that little private world of*
> *dope. She was just too sensitive to survive.*

Billie survived long enough to sing a few days at the Five Spot, a club that opened in downtown New York in the fifties. Her last appearance was at the Phoenix Theater in New York in May 1959. On May 31 she was brought to a hospital unconscious, suffering from liver and heart ailments. Twelve days later someone allegedly found heroin in her room. By now a thin, suffering woman, she was arrested while in her hospital bed and put under police guard. But she escaped the judgment of the United States of America versus Billie Holiday for a higher judgment, on July 17.

The Day Lady Died

> *It is 12:20 in New York a Friday*
> *three days after Bastille day, yes*
> *it is 1959 and I go get a shoeshine*
> *because I will get off the 4:19 in Easthampton*
> *at 7:15 and then go straight to dinner*
> *and I don't know the people who will feed me*
>
> *I walk up the muggy street beginning to sun*

and have a hamburger and a malted and buy
an ugly NEW WORLD WRITING *to see what the poets*
in Ghana are doing these days
                                    I go on to the bank
and Miss Stillwagon (first name Linda I once heard)
doesn't even look up my balance for once in her life
and in the GOLDEN GRIFFIN *I get a little Verlaine*
for Patsy with drawings by Bonnard although I do
think of Hesiod, trans. Richmond Lattimore or
Brendan Behan's new play or Le Balcon *or* Les Nègres
of Genet, but I don't, I stick with Verlaine
after practically going to sleep with quandariness

and for Mike I just stroll into the PARK LANE
Liquor Store and ask for a bottle of Strega and
then I go back where I came from to 6th Avenue
and the tobacconist in the Ziegfield Theatre and
casually ask for a carton of Gauloises and a carton
of Picayunes, and a NEW YORK POST *with her face on it*

and I am sweating a lot by now and thinking of
leaning on the john door in the 5 SPOT
while she whispered a song along the keyboard
to Mal Waldron and everyone and I stopped breathing

                              Frank O'Hara, 1959

5

Aretha Franklin

Her second hit album was called *Aretha Arrives,* and in 1967 when it appeared there was still a great stir over the "arrival" of Aretha Franklin. Her records were selling a million copies each, her picture was on the cover of *Time,* her music had become the subject of endless discussion. Magazines and newspapers featured article after article: This "soul" music— what is it? Where had it come from? Who had "soul" and who didn't? How come Aretha Franklin was such a success?

"Soul," a common term of identification among black people, had first come to national attention in the summer of 1965. In Watts, California, during a riot to protest conditions there, black store owners had chalked "soul brother" on their windows to be spared the violence intended for whites only. By the summer of 1967 many more windows had been smashed, and "soul music"—new, loud, demanding—had drowned out the singing of the nonviolent civil rights movement's anthem, *We Shall Overcome (Someday).* It was another form of Black Power. White people who had listened to spirituals and blues

with sympathy heard Aretha's commanding voice with aston-
ishment. Like the protesters' chant "Freedom *Now,*" it gave no
one time for second thoughts. There had been thought enough,
many black people said, and no action. The militancy of which
soul was a part had been developing for 350 years in America.
That was plenty of time.

Like soul, Aretha Franklin's "arrival" was as much the story
of where she had been. Though most people agreed she was a
fantastic singer, different people responded differently to her
sudden success. For some she'd by no means arrived; on the
contrary, she'd *left.* Others thought she hadn't gone anywhere
at all, that her music was great but not all that new. A lot
depended on what people had been listening to—what radio
stations they played, what records they bought, what their
neighborhood jukebox featured—and where they came from.
Aretha Franklin came from Detroit's East Side, from the New
Bethel Baptist Church where her father was minister, and from
the gospel circuit where she'd been singing and traveling since
she was fourteen. The world into which she arrived, aside from
an occasional ear to Mahalia Jackson and a few other jazz and
popular singers, had not listened to the blues, to black people's
own music, for many years. Bessie Smith had been forgotten.
Billie Holiday's later following had been limited to jazz fans,
and she'd been dead for nearly a decade. But Aretha Franklin
burst right onto the popular music scene, and within a year was
at the very top. The fuss over the arrival of soul in the sixties
was like the excitement over the discovery of blues in the
twenties, but this time there was a catch. After the discussions
were over and the magazine articles filed away, soul was still
African American music. It might be imitated, but it would
never be taken over, as had happened with swing, for instance.
By the sixties black people had come a long way in this coun-

try, musically and otherwise, and if it was soul they had held onto all that while, they had also acquired some resources to defend it.

In 1942, when Aretha was born, the situation was very different. Memphis, Tennessee, her birthplace, was the same South where Bessie Smith had died five years before, and Ma Rainey only three. Nationally, segregation was a fact of life and affected everyone's life. World War II had been on for a year and the armed forces were still segregated; blood donated by whites could not be used to save black lives or vice versa. There were still sections in record catalogues labeled "Race Entertainment." Billie Holiday, age twenty-seven, was singing in New York nightclubs to soldiers she was not permitted to talk to during intermission. Mahalia Jackson, thirty-one, was traveling the country singing gospel music to people she could talk to as well as sing to, the same audiences who had come to hear Bessie and Ma, who had somehow survived the worst of the Depression and would also survive the war.

Aretha was born to a gospel-circuit family. They weren't poor but there were other problems. Her mother, Barbara Siggers, said to have been a talented singer, left the family when Aretha was six and died four years later. Aretha, her two sisters, and two brothers were raised by their father, the Reverend C. L. Franklin. They missed something; as Mahalia Jackson said, "After her Mama died, the whole family wanted for love."

Mr. Franklin moved his family from Memphis to Buffalo, New York, and finally to Detroit when he became minister of New Bethel. He was the first star of the family. Known as "the Man with the Million-Dollar Voice," he was earning $4,000 a sermon in the early fifties and had already produced seventy best-selling recorded sermons by the late sixties. His style was a big influence on his family (Aretha often sang with her sisters, Erma and Carolyn) and on other musicians as well. The Franklins lived in a big house with a lawn and trees, but within what later became known as a northern ghetto (*ghetto* was originally an Italian word for a walled-in section of a city where Jews had to live). Their prosperity did not shield them, as Aretha's brother Cecil explained: "The people that you saw who had any measure of success were the pimp and the hustler, the numbers man and the dope man. Aretha knew what they were all about without having to meet them personally."

As it had for Mahalia, the world of the church provided identification and place for Aretha as a child. Many famous gospel musicians made their way to the Franklin household. Some of the ladies mothered her, "showed her how to take care of herself," though she was described as being "moody and retiring." Aretha, the shy girl in the corner, mostly listened to the music. At about eight or nine she began to try the piano, but when her father hired a woman to teach her Aretha refused: "When she'd come, I'd hide. I tried for maybe a week, but I just couldn't take it. She had all those little baby books, and I wanted to go directly to the tunes." Not long after, gospel singer-composer James Cleveland came to stay with the Franklins and it was from him that Aretha learned the piano: "He showed me some real nice chords and I liked his deep, deep sound. There's a whole lot of earthiness in the way he sings, and what he was feeling, I was feeling, but I just didn't know how to put it across. The more I watched him, the more I got out of it." Cleveland also helped Aretha and her sister Erma form, with two others, a gospel quartet, but it didn't last long ("too busy fussing and fighting," Aretha explained). Aretha's favorite singer was Clara Ward, a good friend of her father and a contemporary of Mahalia Jackson, who would often sing for the Franklin family.

Aretha in concert.

Aretha remembered her inspired spirit at an aunt's funeral—
in the middle of a song Clara pulled off her hat and threw it
on the ground. "That was when I wanted to become a
singer," Aretha told an interviewer. She sang her first solo in
church at age twelve, and from the crowd that gathered after
the service it was clear that Reverend Franklin had another
star in the family. In 1956 Aretha made her first gospel
records, now considered classics, which further established
her reputation.

By the time she was fourteen she was serving her apprentice-
ship, traveling the country as a featured performer in her
father's gospel caravan. She rode hundreds of miles by car,
encountering the usual experiences of a black musician on
tour: "Driving eight or ten hours trying to make a gig, and
being hungry and passing restaurants all along the road, and

having to go off the highway into some little city to find a place to eat because you're black." Aretha traveled for four years. It was not an ideal way to spend one's adolescence. "Trying to grow up is hurting, you know," she said once. "You make mistakes. You try to learn from them, and when you don't it hurts even more." At fifteen she had a son, and then married her manager, Ted White. Before she was out of her teens she had three sons, and later had a fourth.

The late fifties and early sixties, when Aretha was singing gospel, were crucial years for civil rights. The Supreme Court had made important decisions in an attempt to end segregation, and now people were trying to make law become reality. It was the time of bus boycotts and sit-ins, of long marches, the bravery of Dr. Martin Luther King and all the people who followed him. Television had brought America's politics into the living room. Added to the events that shaped Aretha's personal life were those that affected everyone: the sight of soldiers leading black children to school past people who spit at them, the sound of demonstrators singing "We Shall Overcome."

But television had not looked into the ghettos yet, where "We Shall Overcome (someday)" was just another song about the same old story, and only part of the music. The few black musicians who appeared on national radio and on TV in its early days were mostly known, like the Ink Spots, for their vocal technique rather than their music. They didn't sing blues, or even a post-classic version of the blues. Before 1958, black singers who recorded for the major companies did sentimental ballads or novelty songs, which white audiences were believed to prefer. During this time independent companies recorded black music that the major companies wouldn't touch.

But in the vast cities all over America where black people lived, the blues were still sung. Black music included not only gospel and jazz, but a popular music, sometimes called "urban blues," which was largely unknown in the mainstream of American life. Aretha, like many others who grew up in cities, heard as much blues as gospel. Many blues musicians found their way to the Franklin home, too, for musicians invariably knew and appreciated each other; people's paths were always crossing, regardless of the type of music with which they were identified. Many, if not most, black musicians stayed in their communities and played their own music during the forties and fifties. Many who had played jazz successfully to white audiences during the twenties and thirties returned when white musicians began to get the jobs.

In the Kansas City that Count Basie had left (to play the swing that Benny Goodman, white, became king of), in Harlem and South Side Chicago and East Side Detroit, were blues singers whom no one had ever seen on television, singers like B. B. King, Bobby Bland, Sam Cooke. These and many more were the people in Aretha's background when at eighteen she decided to sing something other than gospel music.

By the early sixties there was reason to believe that contemporary black music, known then as "rhythm and blues," could also be sold to white audiences. "Rhythm and blues" was first used in the late forties by one record company as a substitute for the word "Race" in its catalogue (other names tried included "ebony" and "sepia"). Like Race, rhythm and blues came to be the code indicating that the performer was black and recording for a black audience.

As far back as the twenties, it had been common practice for white musicians to "borrow" black music and make records of their own, called "covering" records, which were more widely distributed and usually made more money.

113

Sometimes the music was altered, often just copied. Rhythm and blues was no exception. During the fifties Elvis Presley made a fortune and attracted a large following among young people with his recordings of songs like "Hound Dog," which had first been recorded on a rhythm and blues label by Big Mama Thornton. After Elvis popularized "rock 'n' roll" music (the term came from a song by Chuck Berry, a black singer), there were many groups and a few soloists who successfully sang their own versions of black popular music. After a while, often through the efforts of disc jockeys who urged their radio listeners to buy the originals, a few black rhythm and blues singers began to see some limited success in the pop market too. And there were indications of better times to come. Ray Charles, who first popularized the gospel sound later called soul on rhythm and blues labels, began to be heard a lot even outside the ghettos. So Aretha decided to try her luck at it.

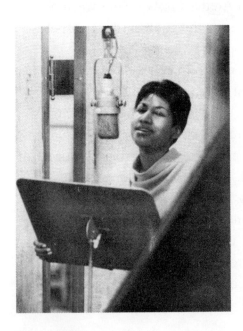

Though in gospel circles singing worldly music isn't usually encouraged, there was no resistance to her decision from Aretha's family. Her father even took her to New York to make her first demonstration records. One of these auditions came to the attention of John Hammond at Columbia, the same man responsible for Bessie's last recordings and Billie's first. Recognizing her talent, Hammond signed Aretha for Columbia, but his original idea to allow her to sing her own music was never carried out—Columbia had become a large corporation and Hammond was only one of many involved. Instead an attempt was made to turn Aretha into a jazz-pop music star, and though she made a few good records, she wasn't herself and she knew it. Nothing seemed right. She got into all sorts of difficulties with agents and managers and was thought to be temperamental. She played nightclubs, unsuccessfully, and later admitted: "I was afraid. I sang to the floor a lot." She appeared at some

jazz festivals, sang at some Caribbean resorts, and then went home to Detroit—owing Columbia money. The attempt seemed to have been a failure and Aretha had to wait until her contract expired before she could try again.

Much happened in the next few years, musically and politically, to pave the way for Aretha's triumph on Atlantic Records in 1967. Into the America already deeply involved in problems of race and identity in the mid-sixties came a series of English musical groups, starting with the Beatles, who also played their own versions of black music. They openly acknowledged the rhythm and blues singers whom they'd copied (they also copied Elvis Presley). These English musicians played what they called "rock" music, and they were able to communicate with their young American audiences in a way that American popular musicians had not done for a long while. Along with folk music in a new style made popular

by Bob Dylan, Joan Baez, and others, rock became a symbol of protest against an older generation whose way of life was considered materially full but spiritually empty. But although folk-rock spurred an interest in rhythm and blues by bringing out men like Chuck Berry and B. B. King, it was quite separate from black popular music. And that still went on, produced and distributed independently.

One independent company, started in 1960, was called Motown Records (after "Motor City," a nickname for Detroit where it began). It featured some solo singers and groups from the same neighborhood as Aretha Franklin. Because of its clearly gospel-influenced beat, the "Motown sound" differed from rock. It would have been hard to mistake the Beatles or the Animals or the Rolling Stones for the Temptations, the Supremes, or Smokey Robinson and the Miracles. Many people preferred the latter, for they saw "Yeah, yeah, yeah" as just another example of borrowed black music-language relaying a fortune into a few white pockets. Though rock musicians credited their sources, they also collected their royalties, and rock was not greeted everywhere with enthusiasm. As Phyl Garland wrote:

> *The relationship of the black listener to the music that he regards as "his" always has been a very deep and personal one, quite often reflecting a great deal about his subordinate position in the society. In contrast to all the things the black man has not had in this country, he has always had "his" music. This has been his special province, and any infringement upon it . . . is likely to be resented.*

The Motown groups, though they appealed to many and were commercially successful, still "belonged" to black audiences. When Martha and the Vandellas sang, "Calling out around the world / Are you ready for a brand-new beat?" black people delighted in the irony. They knew that beat was older than Motown or even the gospel tambourine. The study of Africa and the African American past had made many people aware and proud of themselves as they had not been before. "Black Is Beautiful," read a 1967 poster, "And It's So Beautiful To Be Black." White people, somewhat grudgingly, agreed. But was it then ugly to be white? "Summer's here / We're dancing in the street," sang Martha and the Vandellas. Everyone sat tight, and waited for trouble. Music, like that African drum, could no longer be forbidden, but it could still be feared.

And then Aretha arrived, singing virtually all at once into millions of ears (250,000—one quarter of a million—copies of her first record were sold in two weeks). Her voice was stunning, an incredible energy that flowed and overflowed. Like Bessie Smith, she was right *there.* And behind her was the gospel beat, that "powerful beat" Mahalia Jackson had described, that "rhythm we held on to from slavery days." But Aretha didn't pray like Mahalia for the endurance to make it on through or make you believe her pain as Billie Holiday had. The statement black artists wished to make had changed; the blues had been transfigured by anger and pride. Aretha's music was a celebration. She was "earth mother exhorting, preacher woman denouncing, militant demanding, forgotten woman wailing." She was black, she was beautiful, and she was best. Someone called that time in 1967 "the summer of 'Retha, Rap, and Revolt."

> *You better think*
> *Think about what you're trying to do to me*
> *Think, that your mind gonna let you set me free*

Freedom freedom freedom oh freedom
Freedom yeah freedom

Hey, think about it

The music didn't differ much from gospel, and Aretha was said to be singing the same thing she used to sing in church, substituting "my man" for "my Lord." A few people disapproved of this use of "sacred" music for songs about life. But spirituals had had political meaning, and gospel itself had borrowed from the blues—sacred music was not an African tradition. The music that sang about God also sang about people; the soul that went to church went everywhere else as well. "Before, my soul was tired," an old lady said during the Montgomery, Alabama, bus boycott. "Now my feet may be tired, but my soul is resting."

Though the soul that black people talked about confused many, it soon was seen to be desirable. It seemed to be the answer to some current problems—"an inviting warmth and genuine feeling" versus "the cold, computerized society of today." Yet it wasn't really *explainable.* One magazine printed thirty-two definitions of it, others ran lists of people they thought had it and those they thought didn't. But the final explanation never came. Aretha was given the title Lady, and then Queen of, Soul. Sammy Davis, Jr., introducing her on television, said: "She doesn't *have* soul, she *is* soul." If one had to *be* it, could soul even be acquired? Once, when Louis Armstrong was asked to define swing, he replied: "If you can't feel it, you ain't got it." Though true enough, this was dismissed as an inadequate definition. Similarly, soul made some white people nervous. They frowned on the idea that black people had something that couldn't or wouldn't be defined. But soul, like swing, had to do with feeling, and in music with the feelings black people experienced—"music from the black spirit," was one definition. As such, it couldn't be borrowed without being qualified, and the phrase "blue-eyed soul," tossed around briefly, was never used very much. After a while the quotation marks around "soul" came off, and it became another euphemism for African American.

Yet the search for soul went on, among young white people especially, despite the fact that rock musicians were not going to play soul music. In their rebellion they sought answers in black lifestyle, black culture. But as Godfrey Cambridge once said, "No one can give you black lessons." And to define black as "oppressed" is missing the point. Black is beautiful; oppression would have it be ragged and living in slums. White musi-

cians would have to discover what made up their own spirit, what kind of people they were and how they felt about life, and play that. "That's what soul is about," according to Aretha—"just living and having to get along."

Every year from 1967 through 1975, Aretha Franklin won the Grammy Award for best rhythm and blues performance. People began to call it the "Aretha Award." In 1973 she recorded a brilliant "Moody's Blues," a jazz classic, which was played on all the pop radio stations. Still, her inevitable return to gospel was predicted: "I'm looking for Aretha to come back one of these days," said one gospel musician. "She won't be happy till she does." It took a few years: Aretha was to win her fifteenth Grammy in 1988 for a gospel album she produced herself. Recorded in her father's church in Detroit, it featured not only her own solo performances but duets with her sisters and others, a hundred-voice choir, and sermons, including one by Jesse Jackson. To her this was not a return, but, as she said, a "labor of love."

But going back—to stay—is not a tradition in black music. When Bessie Smith recorded during the thirties, after the years of her immense popularity were over, she would sing only with a newer, swing band. This was to be true of Aretha. After her 1975 Grammy, her career declined. Her explanation seems clear: "I cannot imagine an artist—or anyone creative—who does not have a lull from time to time."

It was a period in which she was apparently happy. Divorced from her first husband, in 1978 she married a second time, to the actor Glynn Turman, and they lived grandly in Hollywood, with her children and his. Aretha continued to make records, but something was missing.

Music changes, as does language, because people change,

and new ones arrive with new and different things to say. There are always transitions. As Aretha herself sang:

This is my same old coat
These are my same old shoes
It was the same old me
With the same old blues

But then you touched my life
Just by holding my hand
When I look in the mirror
I see a brand new girl

To new generations, singing "the same old blues" was part of the past. Soul music's hopes and demands had drifted into dissatisfaction. By the eighties, all America was dancing to disco, some had been through funk, and there were hints in the air of what would later be called rap. Like any artist who persists as a voice to be heard, Aretha came out of her "lull" and in 1981, her fortieth year, won another Grammy, for a fast-paced new version of a song titled "Hold On, I'm Comin'." She followed this success with other popular hits—"Jump to It," "Freeway of Love," and "Who's Zoomin' Who." Millions of people of all races, many of them young and unfamiliar with her soul songs of the sixties, bought recordings of this music and came to her concerts to see her perform it. In 1980 Aretha appeared in *The Blues Brothers,* a film that also featured Ray Charles and "Godfather of Soul" James Brown. Wearing a pink uniform, she plays the owner of a coffee shop and sings her famous song "Think." Like Bessie in her brief movie role, Aretha shines through an otherwise trivial film. Regrettably, she has never chosen to explore her theatrical talents, although in 1984 she almost—before changing her mind—appeared on Broadway in a show based on the life and work of Mahalia Jackson.

Divorced a second time, Aretha returned to her hometown of Detroit and hates to leave it. Awards line the walls of her living room. In 1987—announcing "The doors are open, girls!"—she became the first woman admitted to the Rock & Roll Hall of Fame. Today, after thirty-plus years in music, she sings to all races and generations. With her she brings the past: the sound of blues and gospel, the proud, righteous cry of her own soul "arrival." And having arrived, the Queen of Soul remains, as she was recently described, "a majestic connection to the royal roots of African American culture."

Afterword:
Old Blues and News

By now the music that grew from the blues has a long, wide history. Most modern music reveals its influence, and African American music itself, apart from never "going back," has never stayed still. After ragtime, jazz, swing, bebop, and soul have come funk, disco, rap, and new jack swing. Into these styles are mixed the likes of reggae, ska, zydeco, samba, and Afro-Cuban rooted Latin, to name a few. All this music is ongoing, a significant contribution to international art. The world continually learns from it, too: in Afropop (contemporary African popular music) you might hear jazz or funk; a recent hit Jamaican reggae record is called "Joy and Blues."

Like other structured classical music, the classic blues is still played within its familiar twelve bars. More than two hundred record labels produce it. You can catch it on some radio stations. There are blues bands and blues clubs all over America and elsewhere in the world; jazz bands play blues too. Many in the audience and some onstage are nonblack and young, responding in their turn to what critic Nelson George has called "the bittersweet reality of the blues," its "power to purge the listener of personal demons."

As part of the whole, the female voice in black music has its own distinguished recorded history, which technology has now made widely available. Today, anyone can listen to Billie the way she herself listened to Bessie, and without having to go to a "good time house" to find a phonograph. Most of Billie's original recordings have been reissued on tape and CD. This is true as well for the work of the others in this book.

These five women have a wealth of stylistic descendants who sing classic blues and jazz as well as pop. Choices of style and subject are linked. Billie may have sung "hunger" and "love" like no one else, but in "Strange Fruit" she also sang about lynching—because jazz can accommodate all three. Contemporary performers, too, must make choices. Singers of classic blues usually interpret familiar pieces, called "standards," from a varied inherited repertoire. (Ruth Brown is a good example.) Jazz singers like Abbey Lincoln either choose new compositions written in known forms or, like blues singers, add their interpretations to standards that already have a history.

Pop music, a very broad description, has included many talented singers—the list is long, from the venerable Ella Fitzgerald to the contemporary Whitney Houston. Although a lot of pop music is trivial and forgettable, much of its impact depends on who plays it. Billie could triumph over slight material because, with others of her generation, she chose to make a statement by taking music in new directions. Today, many pop singers are "crossover" artists, produced by large corporations according to established, commercially successful formulas. Whitney Houston, for example, uses her gospel-inspired voice to describe a narrower, more ideal, and less gritty range of experience (though at a concert in 1993 she did sing some standards, including "I Loves You Porgy," which Billie and others have performed). What if she were to leave what one reviewer has called "the gilded cage of pop mega-stardom"? In music anything is possible, and change in African American music is inevitable.

As people are part of their time, they are part of their place. Well into the sixties, to record, press, and distribute a record to local radio stations cost about five hundred dollars. In many American cities, independent record companies based in black communities continually discovered and introduced local talent. The music unique to that place then reached all of us, in time. Today, although it's still customary to look for new music among the people who first sang blues, in their economically depressed communities there are fewer small companies to promote and encourage it.

New black music nevertheless reaches out. Rap, its most noticeably new form, was first produced by young people in New York. As Tricia Rose explains in her book *Black Noise*, rap first appeared in the seventies, as one part of hip-hop, "an African-American and Afro-Caribbean youth culture composed of graffiti, breakdancing, and rap music." (Though the terms hip-hop and rap are often used interchangeably to refer to the music, hip-hop best explains the entire culture, including styles, while the term rap refers only to the music.) Rap began as a disk jockey invention, with the person spinning the records at a dance talking (rapping) over parts of the music he was playing. (Deejays in Jamaica had done this earlier, and rappers also learned from the artful, rhythmic delivery of some rhythm and blues radio announcers.) Like blues, or any music that has a vocal part, rap has developed a structure. Like modern jazz—which once aroused complaints of "Where's the melody?"—rap downplays the melodic aspect of music for rhythms best described as "expect the unexpected." Rap rhymes are inventive; its lyrics have progressed from good-humored party encouragement to statements of urban frustration to those of "gangsta" rap—angry, crude, cruel, and often demeaning to women. Rap's defenders claim it's exactly what it wants to be: the voice of a disaffected generation who feel stuck and shortchanged, young people describing what Mahalia called the "burden of being a colored person in the white man's world." But critics are challenging rap's sometimes violent solutions.

127

As the writer Rosalyn M. Story points out, something has gone "desperately awry" between Aretha Franklin's proud rendition of "Respect," and the rap by 2 Live Crew called "Pop that Coochie." Nevertheless, like every other black American musical style, rap has been widely copied—not only in English. And though most rappers are men, among them are women such as Queen Latifah and MC Lyte, who speak from a strong, challenging female perspective. Efforts have been made to put rap to good use, to clean up its act. But it has already made its points.

Given the inevitability of *next* in black music, what will it be? What places will it come from, what will it want to say? Racism, along with the necessary struggle against it, continues even as this singable, danceable, sacred, serious music continues creating itself and inspiring others. Music is much more than struggle, but while struggle exists that will be in it.

At the turn of a century people often pause to assess the past and restate the future. As the nineteenth became the twentieth, Ma Rainey sang, "I done bought my ticket, but I don't know where I'm going." At that moment, the blues involved *all* Americans in African American music. Both blacks and whites, in some way, were part of the life it referred to. As the twentieth century becomes the twenty-first, the uncertainty voiced by Ma Rainey has been echoed and reechoed. If the life that rap describes is unacceptable, this, too, involves all Americans. New music, as it has before, will find a new way to say what must be said.

The question, finally, is who will be listening. In 1925, when the white writer-photographer Carl Van Vechten went to Newark to hear Bessie Smith sing, her voice, though beautiful, was foreign to him. So were the people in the audience, who astonished him by bursting into "hysterical semi-religious shrieks of sorrow and lamentation." Half a century later, in the seventies, it would have been hard to sort out by race the tremendous response when Aretha Franklin, at the end of a concert at Madison Square Garden, said to a mixed audience: "You didn't think I was going to leave without playing the blues, did you?" By then, blood to save American lives was no longer kept in separate containers, as it had been the year of her birth. As she once put it: "Everybody who's living has problems and desires. . . . When we cry, we're all gonna cry tears, and when we laugh, we have to smile."

This is no less true now, though our segregated lives keep us out of sight of each other, if not out of earshot. While it is common to look to black people for new music, it is also a pattern to overlook what inspires it. Change, though inevitable musically, must be willed socially, and by all of us listening. Because this, as Aretha sang, is where we all live:

> *This is the house that Jack built, y'all,*
> *Remember this house.*
> *This was the land that he worked by hand*
> *This was the dream of an upright man*
>
> *The house that Jack built*
> *Oh remember this house.*

Selected Bibliography

The following, with a few exceptions, are all current paperbacks. Some are new works; others are reprints of classic books on blues and jazz.

Albertson, Chris. *Bessie.* New York: Stein and Day, 1972.

Armstrong, Louis. *Satchmo: My Life in New Orleans.* New York: Prentice Hall, 1954. Paperback reissue, New York: Da Capo Press, 1986.

Baraka, Amiri (LeRoi Jones). *Blues People.* New York: William Morrow and Co., 1963.

Bego, Mark. *Aretha Franklin, The Queen of Soul.* New York: St. Martin's Press, 1989.

Charters, Samuel. *The Legacy of the Blues.* London: Calder & Boyars, Ltd., 1975. Paperback reissue, New York: Da Capo Press, 1977.

————. *The Roots of the Blues.* Boston: Marion Boyars, Inc., 1981. Paperback reissue, New York: Da Capo Press, 1991.

————, and Leonard Kunstadt. *Jazz: A History of the New York Scene.* Garden City, New York: Doubleday and Co.,

1962. Paperback reissue, New York: Da Capo Press, 1981.

Chilton, John. *Billie's Blues: The Billie Holiday Story 1933–1959.* New York: Stein and Day, 1975. Paperback reissue, New York: Da Capo Press, 1989.

Donloe, Darlene. *Mahalia Jackson.* Los Angeles: Melrose Square Publishing Company, 1992.

Feather, Leonard. *Encyclopedia of Jazz.* New York: Horizon Press, 1966. Paperback reissue, New York: Da Capo Press, 1984.

Fox, Ted. *Showtime at the Apollo.* New York: Holt, Rinehart and Winston, 1983. Paperback reissue, New York: Da Capo Press, 1993.

Garon, Paul and Beth. *Woman With Guitar: Memphis Minnie's Blues.* New York: Da Capo Press, 1992.

George, Nelson. *The Death of Rhythm and Blues.* New York: E.P. Dutton, 1989.

———. *Where Did Our Love Go: The Rise and Fall of the Motown Sound.* New York: St. Martin's Press, 1985.

Giddins, Gary. *Satchmo.* New York: Anchor Books, 1988.

Gillett, Charlie. *The Sound of the City.* New York: Pantheon Books, 1983.

Guralnick, Peter. *Sweet Soul Music.* New York: Harper Perennial, 1986.

Haralambos, Michael. *Soul Music: The Birth of a Sound in Black America.* New York: Paperback reissue, Da Capo Press, 1985. First published as *Right On! From Blues to Soul in Black America.* London: Eddison Press, Ltd, 1974.

Harris, Michael W. *The Rise of Gospel Blues.* New York: Oxford University Press, 1992.

Harrison, Daphne Duval. *Black Pearls: Blues Queens of the*

1920s. New Brunswick, N.J.: Rutgers University Press, 1988.

Haskins, James. *Black Music in America: A History Through Its People*. New York: HarperCollins, 1987.

Heilbut, Anthony. *The Gospel Sound*. New York: Simon and Schuster, 1971. Revised and updated edition, New York: Limelight Editions, 1992.

Hentoff, Nat, and Nat Shapiro, eds. *Hear Me Talkin' To Ya*. New York: Dover Books, 1966.

Holiday, Billie, with William F. Dufty. *Lady Sings the Blues*. New York: Doubleday and Co., 1956. Paperback reissue, New York: Penguin, 1992.

Howard, Brett. *Lena Horne*. Los Angeles: Melrose Square Publishing Company, 1981.

Hughes, Langston, and Milton Meltzer. *Black Magic: A Pictorial History of the African-American in the Performing Arts*. Paperback reissue, New York: Da Capo Press, 1990. First published as *Black Magic: A Pictorial History of the Negro in American Entertainment*. New York: Prentice Hall, 1967.

Jackson, Mahalia, with Evan McLeod Wylie. *Movin' On Up*. New York: Hawthorn Books, 1966.

Keil, Charles. *Urban Blues*. Chicago: University of Chicago Press, 1966.

Kliment, Bud. *Ella Fitzgerald*. Los Angeles: Melrose Square Publishing Company, 1989.

Murray, Albert. *Stomping the Blues*. New York: McGraw-Hill, 1976. Paperback reissue, New York: Da Capo Press, 1989.

Oliver, Paul. *Blues Fell This Morning*. New York: Cambridge University Press, 2nd edition, 1990.

O'Meally, Robert. *Lady Day: The Many Faces of Billie Holi-*

day. New York: Arcade Publishing, a Little, Brown company, 1991. Adapted as film for television and videocassette by Kultur International Films Ltd.

Palmer, Robert. *Deep Blues.* New York: Penguin, 1982.

Schuller, Gunther. *Early Jazz.* New York: Oxford University Press, 1966.

Sidran, Ben. *Black Talk.* New York: Holt, Rinehart and Winston, 1971. Paperback reissue, New York: Da Capo Press, 1983.

Stearns, Marshall. *The Story of Jazz.* New York: Oxford University Press, 1962.

Stewart-Baxter, Derrick. *Ma Rainey and the Classic Blues Singers.* New York: Stein and Day, 1970.

Waldo, Terry. *This Is Ragtime.* New York: Hawthorn Books, 1976. Paperback reissue, New York: Da Capo Press, 1991.

Waters, Ethel, with Charles Samuels. *His Eye Is on the Sparrow.* New York: Doubleday and Co., 1950. Paperback reissue, New York: Da Capo Press, 1992.

Williams, Martin T. *The Art of Jazz.* New York: Oxford University Press, 1959.

Selected Discography

Below are only a few of the hundreds of blues and jazz recordings that are now available on CD and cassette. All are new collections assembled from the original material.

The Essential Spirituals (Columbia 4737882), CD.
*Sounds of the South: A Musical Journey from the Georgia Sea
    Islands to the Mississippi Delta.* Recorded in the field.
    (Atlantic 7 82496-2), four-CD set.
Blues with a Feeling (Vanguard Records VCD 2-77005), CD.
Blues Masters: The Essential Blues Collection, 12 volumes
    (Rhino Records R471121-35), particularly Classic Blues
    Women (R471134) and Urban Blues (R471121), CD or
    cassette.
Atlantic Blues, 4 volumes (782309-2) CD, (781694-7) cas-
    sette.
New Orleans Ladies (Rounder C-2078), cassette.
Louis Armstrong & the Singers 1924/30, 4 volumes (King Jazz
    KJ 139-142FS), four CDs.
The Smithsonian Collection of Classic Jazz, volume I revised
    (RD033-1/ A21730), CD.

The Great Tomato Blues Package (Music Works, Rhino Records, R270386), two-CD set.

Roots n' Blues: The Retrospective 1925–1950, (Columbia/ Legacy 47911), CD or cassette.

Chess Blues: 1001 Song Retrospective 1947–67 (MCA/Chess CHD4-9340), four-CD set.

The Okeh Rhythm & Blues Story 1949–1957 (Epic/OK/Legacy 48912), three CDs or cassettes.

Ma Rainey

Ma Rainey's Black Bottom (Yazoo 1071), CD.

Ma Rainey (Milestone MCD-47021-2), CD.

"Ma" Rainey: The Paramounts (Black Swan HCD-12002), two-CD set.

Bessie Smith

Bessie Smith: The Complete Recordings in 4 Volumes (Columbia/ Legacy C2K47091, C2K47471, C2K47474, C2K52838), eight CDs or cassettes.

Bessie Smith 1925–1933 (Hermes HRM 6003), CD or cassette.

Bessie Smith Sings the Jazz (Jazz Archives N61), CD or cassette.

Mahalia Jackson

Mahalia Jackson's Greatest Hits (Columbia PCT 37710), cassette.

Mahalia Jackson: Gospel, Spirituals & Hymns, 2 volumes (Columbia/Legacy C2K47083, C2K48924), four-CD set.

Billie Holiday

Billie Holiday: The Legacy (Columbia/Legacy 47724), three CDs.

The Complete Billie Holiday on Verve 1945–1959 (Verve 314517638-2), ten-CD set.

Billie Holiday (Commodore Records CCD70011), CD.

Billie Holiday: The Complete Decca Recordings (Decca GRD2601), two CDs.

There are also a number of single CDs and cassette tapes of Billie Holiday recordings.

Aretha Franklin

Aretha Franklin's 30 Greatest Hits (Atlantic 781668-2), CD.

The Best of Aretha Franklin (Atlantic 81280-2), CD or cassette.

Aretha Sings the Blues (Columbia 40105), CD or cassette.

Aretha Franklin: Jazz to Soul (Columbia/Legacy C2K48515), two CDs.

Queen of Soul: The Atlantic Records (Rhino Records 71063), four CDs or cassettes.

Amazing Grace (Atlantic CS2-906), CD.

There are also a number of single CDs and cassette tapes of Aretha Franklin recordings.

Other Notable Women in Black Music

BETTY CARTER (1930–). Made her professional debut in 1946; was once known as Betty "Be-Bop"; is now a well-known jazz improviser with a unique, brooding lyricism.

IDA COX (1889–1967). Did most of her recording during the height of the blues craze; also toured during the thirties and recorded as late as 1961. Sometimes called the Uncrowned Queen of the Blues.

ELLA FITZGERALD (1918–). Began singing in the mid-thirties, mostly popular music; soon achieved a wide reputation for her clarity and rhythmic accomplishments. One of the best-known female vocalists of the twentieth century.

BERTHA "CHIPPIE" HILL (1905–1950). Recorded in the twenties; was "rediscovered" in the late forties and appeared in nightclubs, at jazz festivals and in concerts.

LENA HORNE (1917–). Started as a dancer at the Cotton Club in Harlem in 1934; became popular singing at Cafe Society. A popular rather than a jazz singer; has appeared in movies and Broadway shows, and on television.

ALBERTA HUNTER (1897–1984). Composer as well as singer; recorded with jazz names; toured during World War II; became a nurse in the fifties; then had a second, successful singing career that lasted until her death.

ABBEY LINCOLN (1930–). Began as a pop singer; toured with a dance band while still in her teens, then worked in clubs; made movies; became a jazz singer in the late fifties. Now one of the premier jazz stylists.

CARMEN McRAE (1922–1994). Began recording in the 1940s; worked as pianist-singer at Minton's. Became one of the most original song stylists of the fifties and appeared at many festivals and in nightclubs.

ODETTA (1930–   ). Started singing folk songs, accompanying herself on guitar, as a hobby. Has appeared at festivals, in concerts and clubs. Sings mainly blues, work songs, ballads, and some classical pop.

NINA SIMONE (1933–   ). Studied and taught piano, attended the Juilliard School and worked as an accompanist, before beginning her own singing career. First hit record in 1959. Also a composer; has been called the High Priestess of Soul.

CLARA SMITH (1895?–1935). The "Queen of the Moaners"; recorded duets with Bessie Smith, toured and recorded on her own during the twenties.

MAMIE SMITH (1890–1946). First recorded black singer. Made many records during the twenties, and toured with her own band, Mamie Smith's Jazz Hounds.

SARAH VAUGHAN (1924–1990). Began career by winning a talent contest at the Apollo Theater; was engaged to sing with the Earl Hines band there in 1943; made her first recording in 1944. Worked nightclubs and in concert. Notable for her unique style and rich tone. Won many awards and recorded extensively.

SIPPIE WALLACE (1899–1952). Known as the Texas Nightingale; toured for many years; was from a musical family; played fine blues piano. One of the best of the twenties.

DINAH WASHINGTON (1924–1963). Started as a pianist with a church choir; by 1943 had made her recording debut, and by 1946 was considered one of the most important rhythm and blues stars of the decade. Her style, combining blues with elements of church sound, influenced many. She also recorded pop tunes, but was known as Queen of the Blues.

ETHEL WATERS (1900–1977). An actress-singer whose career spanned the twentieth century; began singing in church at five and was known as Sweet Mama Stringbean when a young woman. Appeared in many Broadway shows and movies; was an internationally known star.

Acknowledgments

(continued from copyright page)

Acknowledgment to Biograph Records, Inc., for permission to reprint lyrics of "Soon This Morning" and "Countin' the Blues."

From *A Treasury of the Blues* by W. C. Handy. Used by permission of Mrs. Charles Boni, executrix of the estate of the publisher, Charles Boni.

"The Day Lady Died," from *Lunch Poems* by Frank O'Hara. Copyright © 1964 by Frank O'Hara. Reprinted by permission of City Lights Books.

From "The House That Jack Built" by Bob Lance and Fran Robbins. Copyright © 1968 by Cotillion Music, Inc., 1841 Broadway, New York, N.Y. 10023. International copyright secured. All rights reserved.

From *Lena* by Lena Horne. Copyright © 1965 by Lena Horne and Richard Shickel. Used by permission of Doubleday & Company, Inc.

From *Lady Sings the Blues* by Billie Holiday. Copyright © 1956 by Eleanora Fagan and William E. Dufty. Used by permission of Doubleday & Company, Inc.

From "Sister Soul" by Phyl Garland. Reprinted by permission of *Ebony* magazine, copyright © 1967 by Johnson Publishing Company, Inc.

From "Wasted Life Blues," words and music by Bessie Smith. Copyright © 1929 Empress Music Inc. Copyright © renewal effective 1957 Empress Music Inc.

From "Think" by Aretha Franklin and Ted White. Copyright © 1968 Fourteenth Hour Music, Inc. Reprinted by permission of the publishers.

From *American Negro Folk Songs* by Newman I. White. Published in 1928 by Harvard University Press. Used by permission.

From *Movin' On Up* by Mahalia Jackson with Evan McLeod Wylie. Copyright © 1966 by Mahalia Jackson and Evan McLeod Wylie. Reprinted by permission of Hawthorn Books, Inc.

From "Take My Hand, Precious Lord." Copyright © 1938 by Hill and Range Songs, Inc. Copyright renewed © 1965 and assigned to Hill & Range Songs, Inc. Used by permission.

Photo Credits

Atlantic Records, 106. Chicago Historical Society, 11, 22. Columbia Records/Don Hunstein, 16, 48–49, 53, 56, 68, 69, 75, 90, 95, 96, 97, 111, 114, 115, 116. Frank Driggs/ Photo Files, 32, 44, 78. *Ebony* magazine, 39, 120. Harvard Theater Collection, 6, 7. Museum of the City of New York, 13, 52, 83. New York Public Library, vii, 103.

Index

About the Author

Hettie Jones lives in New York City, where she writes and teaches. She is the author of several books for children and young adults, as well as the Beat memoir *How I Became Hettie Jones* (Dutton and Penguin). A poet as well as a prose writer, over the years Ms. Jones has read her work at many venues, from cafés to colleges. She is currently planning a history of African American women composers.